LUKE

REFORMED EXPOSITORY BIBLE STUDIES

A Companion Series to the Reformed Expository Commentaries

Series Editors

Daniel M. Doriani
Iain M. Duguid
Richard D. Phillips
Philip Graham Ryken

1 Samuel: A King after God's Own Heart
Esther & Ruth: The Lord Delivers and Redeems
Daniel: Faith Enduring through Adversity
Matthew: Making Disciples for the Nations (two volumes)
Luke: Knowing for Sure (two volumes)
Galatians: The Gospel of Free Grace
Ephesians: The Glory of Christ in the Life of the Church
Hebrews: Standing Firm in Christ
James: Portrait of a Living Faith

Coming in 2022

Song of Songs: Friendship on Fire
John: The Word Incarnate (two volumes)
Philippians: To Live Is Christ

LUKE

KNOWING FOR SURE
Volume 1 (Chapters 1–10)

A 13-LESSON STUDY

REFORMED EXPOSITORY
BIBLE STUDY

JON NIELSON
and **PHILIP GRAHAM RYKEN**

P&R PUBLISHING
P.O. BOX 817 • PHILLIPSBURG • NEW JERSEY 08865-0817

Scripture quotations are from the ESV® Bible (The Holy Bible, English Standard Version®), copyright © 2001 by Crossway, a publishing ministry of Good News Publishers. Used by permission. All rights reserved.

All boxed quotations are taken from Philip Graham Ryken's *Luke*, vol. 1, in the Reformed Expository Commentary series. Page numbers in quotations refer to that source.

ISBN: 978-1-62995-841-5 (pbk)
ISBN: 978-1-62995-842-2 (ePub)

Printed in the United States of America

CONTENTS

SERIES INTRODUCTION

Studying the Bible will change your life. This is the consistent witness of Scripture and the experience of people all over the world, in every period of church history.

King David said, "The law of the LORD is perfect, reviving the soul; the testimony of the LORD is sure, making wise the simple; the precepts of the LORD are right, rejoicing the heart; the commandment of the LORD is pure, enlightening the eyes" (Ps. 19:7–8). So anyone who wants to be wiser and happier, and who wants to feel more alive, with a clearer perception of spiritual reality, should study the Scriptures.

Whether we study the Bible alone or with other Christians, it will change us from the inside out. The Reformed Expository Bible Studies provide tools for biblical transformation. Written as a companion to the Reformed Expository Commentary, this series of short books for personal or group study is designed to help people study the Bible for themselves, understand its message, and then apply its truths to daily life.

Each Bible study is introduced by a pastor-scholar who has written a full-length expository commentary on the same book of the Bible. The individual chapters start with the summary of a Bible passage, explaining **The Big Picture** of this portion of God's Word. Then the questions in **Getting Started** introduce one or two of the passage's main themes in ways that connect to life experience. These questions may be especially helpful for group leaders in generating lively conversation.

Understanding the Bible's message starts with seeing what is actually there, which is where **Observing the Text** comes in. Then the Bible study provides a longer and more in-depth set of questions entitled **Understanding the Text**. These questions carefully guide students through the entire passage, verse by verse or section by section.

It is important not to read a Bible passage in isolation, but to see it in the wider context of Scripture. So each Bible study includes two **Bible Connections** questions that invite readers to investigate passages from other places in Scripture—passages that add important background, offer valuable contrasts or comparisons, and especially connect the main passage to the person and work of Jesus Christ.

The next section is one of the most distinctive features of the Reformed Expository Bible Studies. The authors believe that the Bible teaches important doctrines of the Christian faith, and that reading biblical literature is enhanced when we know something about its underlying theology. The questions in **Theology Connections** identify some of these doctrines by bringing the Bible passage into conversation with creeds and confessions from the Reformed tradition, as well as with learned theologians of the church.

Our aim in all of this is to help ordinary Christians apply biblical truth to daily life. **Applying the Text** uses open-ended questions to get people thinking about sins that need to be confessed, attitudes that need to change, and areas of new obedience that need to come alive by the power and influence of the Holy Spirit. Finally, each study ends with a **Prayer Prompt** that invites Bible students to respond to what they are learning with petitions for God's help and words of praise and gratitude.

You will notice boxed quotations throughout the Bible study. These quotations come from one of the volumes in the Reformed Expository Commentary. Although the Bible study can stand alone and includes everything you need for a life-changing encounter with a book of the Bible, it is also intended to serve as a companion to a full commentary on the same biblical book. Reading the full commentary is especially useful for teachers who want to help their students answer the questions in the Bible study at a deeper level, as well as for students who wish to further enrich their own biblical understanding.

The people who worked together to produce this series of Bible studies have prayed that they will engage you more intimately with Scripture, producing the kind of spiritual transformation that only the Bible can bring.

Philip Graham Ryken
Coeditor of the Reformed Expository Commentary series
Author of *Luke* (REC)

INTRODUCING LUKE

Luke is the third and longest of the biblical Gospels. Its **main purpose** is to provide a true and orderly account of Christ's life, ministry, sufferings, death, and resurrection so that people who read the book "may have certainty concerning the things" (Luke 1:4) that it teaches about the Savior who came "to seek and to save the lost" (19:10). In other words, the gospel of Luke was written to strengthen our faith in Jesus and to give us greater assurance of the salvation he brings.

"The Gospel of Knowing for Sure," as we might call it, is named for the man who wrote it: "Luke the beloved physician" (Col. 4:14). Dr. Luke, who accompanied the apostle Paul on some of his famous missionary journeys, happens to be the only New Testament **author** who was not a Jew but a Greek. His careful attention to detail, tender compassion for people who suffer, and evident fascination with healing miracles all reflect his calling to the medical profession. Like many good Christian doctors, Luke was an everyday evangelist who wanted everyone he met to know more about Jesus. A gifted historian as well as a skilled physician, he penned not one but two best sellers—the New Testament book of Acts also bears his signature. In his gospel, Luke wrote down "all that Jesus began to do and teach" (Acts 1:1). Then, in the book of Acts, he told the rest of the story, portraying the good news of Jesus Christ being proclaimed all over the world through the power of the Holy Spirit.

Luke addressed both his gospel and its sequel to a person whom he calls "most excellent Theophilus" (Luke 1:3; see also Acts 1:1). Because he is given this honorific title ("most excellent"), some notable scholars maintain that Theophilus was a high-ranking Roman official. Since Luke's purpose behind what he wrote to Theophilus was to give greater assurance concerning the truth about Jesus, presumably this important leader was at least somewhat familiar with Christianity but wanted to learn more. Others believe that Luke wrote for Theophilus the son of Ananias, who became high priest in Jerusalem several years after Jesus died and rose again. But even though he was writing to a specific individual, Luke also had a more general **audience** in mind. The name *Theophilus* means "friend of God" or "lover of God." If we are friends of God through our loving faith in Jesus Christ, then this gospel was written for us as much as it was written for anyone.

Our understanding of Luke's audience makes a difference regarding how we understand the book's **context**. Was Luke writing to a Jew or a Gentile? To a religious leader in Jerusalem or to a Roman official in a city like Antioch—or even Rome itself? When we read this gospel, we discover that Luke provides sufficient information about daily life in ancient Galilee and religious customs in biblical Jerusalem for us to be able to understand Christ's life and ministry within their original setting.

Luke begins his account of Christ's public ministry with Jesus's first sermon, which he preached at his hometown synagogue in Nazareth. The book's **key verse** comes from Jesus's quotation from the Old Testament book of Isaiah: "The Spirit of the Lord is upon me, because he has anointed me to proclaim good news to the poor. He has sent me to proclaim liberty to the captives and recovering of sight to the blind, to set at liberty those who are oppressed, to proclaim the year of the Lord's favor" (Luke 4:18–19; cf. Isa. 61:1–2). Once he had read these words aloud, Jesus sat down and calmly said, "Today this Scripture has been fulfilled in your hearing" (Luke 4:21). By saying this, he was claiming to be the Savior whom God had always promised to send—the one who would preach good news to poor sinners and would bring healing for every wound and freedom from every form of bondage. As the rest of the gospel story unfolds, we will see Jesus actively carry out the exact kind of ministry that Isaiah foretold—one that was "mighty in deed and word" (24:19). He will heal the sick, give sight to the blind, set captives free from spiritual bondage, and—most of all—preach the good news of forgiveness for sin.

Many scholars have identified spiritual themes and specific episodes within the life of Christ that are unique to Luke's gospel. Luke gives us the fullest account of Jesus's birth and boyhood—one that includes four of the first Christmas carols. Of the gospel writers, he provides the most complete record of the healing ministry that Jesus exhibited as the Great

Physician. He tells more stories about forgiveness and places a special focus on prayer—eleven of the fifteen prayers of Jesus that are recorded in the Bible are included in Luke's gospel. He also retells nearly twenty parables about the kingdom of God that do not appear in the gospels of Matthew, Mark, or John—including many that deal with the stewardship of money and treat it as an important spiritual issue. And he takes special notice of the women who supported Jesus and were blessed by his ministry.[1]

As we encounter these varied episodes from the life of Christ, what **theological themes** can we discern within Luke's gospel? By providing the fullest account of our Savior's nativity—which includes the beautiful songs that men, women, and angels sang to celebrate his miraculous birth in Bethlehem—this gospel helps us to understand the mystery of the *incarnation*. Luke's down-to-earth presentation of the life of Christ generally emphasizes our Savior's humanity. But, paradoxically, his favorite title for Jesus—"Son of Man"—is an Old Testament term that bears witness to his deity.

Luke has even more to say about the death of Christ than he does about the birth of Christ. As do the other gospels, this one pays disproportionate attention to the last week of our Savior's life, when unrelenting opposition to his ministry intensified his sufferings and resulted in his bloody crucifixion. Luke wants us to understand the doctrine of the *atonement*—the truth that, by dying in our place, Jesus paid the price of our sins and reconciled us to God.

We should also see Luke as a theologian of the Holy Spirit—especially when we take into account the second part of his two-volume masterpiece: the book of Acts. The good doctor was interested in what theologians call *pneumatology*: the study of the person and work of the third member of the Trinity. From the moment he was baptized in the Jordan River through the moment he walked out of the empty tomb, Jesus was empowered by the Holy Spirit.

One more area to mention that Luke's theology encompasses is *missiology*, which relates to the church's calling to proclaim the gospel to the

---

1. In order to maximize the time we spend on some of the passages and episodes that are unique to Luke's gospel and tied to these central themes, this study will not include an in-depth examination of *every* passage in the book. At times, you will be encouraged to read some sections of his gospel without answering specific questions about them.

whole world. During his life on earth, Jesus preached the good news to as many needy people as he could: poor shepherds, lonely widows, crooked businessmen, despised lepers, and foreigners who were outside the family of faith. As he reached out to people who were lost, Jesus was beginning to fulfill the prophecy that had been issued at his birth that he would bring salvation to "all peoples"—to Gentiles as well as to Jews (2:31; see also 32). This work would continue through his disciples, whom he commissioned to preach "repentance for the forgiveness of sins . . . to all nations, beginning from Jerusalem" (24:47).

Every aspect of Luke's theology is designed not only to give us greater certainty about Christ's saving work but also to draw us deeper into the life of costly Christian discipleship. The most important **practical application** of his gospel we can make is simply to trust its message of salvation and to believe in Jesus. But that is not Luke's only objective for us: he also wants us to take up our crosses and follow Jesus.

One of Luke's favorite literary and pastoral techniques is to set two characters in contrast in order to demonstrate the true and best way to follow Jesus. Luke gives us two dinner guests, Simon and a sinful woman, along with opposite assessments of their spiritual condition (see 7:36–50); two sisters, Mary and Martha, who take different postures toward spiritual instruction (see 10:38–42); two brothers, younger and older, who were both far from their father's heart—but in very different ways (see 15:11–32); two neighbors from two different tax brackets, the rich man and poor Lazarus, who reached totally different eternal destinations (16:19–31); two men who went to the temple to pray, a Pharisee and a tax collector—only one of whom had a right standing with God (18:9–14); and so on.

True Christian disciples care for the same kinds of people whom Jesus treated with compassion. And if our Savior was both a healer of the body and a physician of the soul, then we too are called both to meet the material needs of our neighbors and to share the good news that may lead them to eternal life. By showing us how completely Jesus transformed the lives of the people he saved—how he liberated many people who were marginalized, oppressed, and underprivileged—Luke helps us to see the social implications of the gospel. The Savior whose miracles demonstrated his power over demons, disease, death, and the devil also calls us to see salvation in all its dimensions and to seek the lost by becoming the friends of sinners.

The gospel of Luke is not some tightly organized treatise but an evangelistic biography that tells many different stories about Jesus. Simply by reading the book from beginning to end, we get drawn into the narrative flow of the birth, life, ministry, sufferings, death, and triumphant resurrection of Jesus. But Luke also leaves us some clues to the fact that he has given careful thought to his book's structure. A crucial moment comes near the end of chapter 9, where Luke tells us that "when the days drew near for [Jesus] to be taken up, he set his face to go to Jerusalem" (v. 51). From that point forward, Christ resolutely set his course toward the cross.

The overall movement of the book is also indicated by Jesus's statement of purpose to Zacchaeus the tax collector: "The Son of Man came to seek and to save the lost" (Luke 19:10). We see Jesus *seeking* the lost from the beginning of his public ministry, when he seeks out his first disciples and begins preaching the good news of the kingdom to the lost souls of Israel. The stories we see in chapter 15 about the lost sheep, the lost coin, and the lost sons are really about his loving pursuit of every lost sinner. By the end of Luke's gospel we also see Jesus *saving* the lost—specifically by dying for their sins and rising again. We catch an early glimpse of this saving work when he tells Zacchaeus, "Today salvation has come to this house" (19:9). And his salvation is more fully displayed on the cross, when he welcomes the thief who is dying on the cross next to him into paradise (see 23:32–43). As we read these gospel stories, Jesus is looking to find us, too—and then to save us forever.

With these key moments in mind, here is one helpful way for us to **outline** the gospel of Luke:

Prologue: Luke's Purpose (1:1–4)

The Advent of the Son of Man
    Birth of Jesus (1:5–2:21)
    Boyhood of Jesus (2:22–52)
    Baptism of Jesus (3:1–38)
    Temptation of Jesus (4:1–13)

The Ministry of the Son of Man
    Jesus Begins His Ministry (4:14–44)

Jesus Calls His Disciples (5:1–6:16)
Jesus Teaches and Performs Miracles (6:17–8:56)
Jesus Commissions His Disciples (9:1–50)

The Mission of the Son of Man on his Way to the Cross
Jesus in Samaria (9:51–10:37)
Jesus in Bethany and Judea (10:38–13:21)
Jesus Journeys to Jerusalem (13:22–17:10)
Jesus between Samaria and Galilee (17:11–18:34)
Jesus near Jericho (18:35–19:27)

The Death of the Son of Man
Triumphal Entry (19:28–44)
Temple Discourses (19:45–21:38)
Last Supper (22:1–38)
Betrayal, Arrest, and Trials (22:39–23:25)
Crucifixion and Burial (23:26–56)

The Triumph of the Son of Man
Resurrection Day (24:1–49)
Ascension Day (24:50–53)

Philip Graham Ryken
Coeditor of the Reformed Expository Commentary series
Coeditor of the Reformed Expository Bible Study series
Author of *Luke* (REC)

LESSON 1

THE FORERUNNER

Luke 1:1-25

THE BIG PICTURE

Luke's gospel begins with introductory remarks that are addressed to "Theophilus"—most likely a wealthy patron of Luke as well as of the ministry of the gospel in the first century (1:3). The name itself means "lover of God," however, and in that sense is widely applicable (perhaps intentionally so) to anyone who reads Luke's gospel with a desire to be more "certain" of the things they have heard (and believed) about God's Son, Jesus Christ (1:4). That is precisely Luke's stated purpose for writing this gospel: he writes as a historian and carefully records the *historical facts* that have been gathered from eyewitnesses about what Jesus Christ did and taught (1:1–2). But Luke's fact-based account is not without spiritual purpose; he wants Theophilus, and all lovers of God, to know for sure that everything he reports about Jesus is true—as well as consistent with what they have already been taught about him (1:4).

The remainder of the passage you will study in this lesson portrays the birth account of John the Baptist—the promised forerunner of the Messiah, Jesus Christ. The angel Gabriel comes to a priest named Zechariah and announces that God will grant a son to his barren wife, Elizabeth (1:5–17). Massive promises accompany the announcement of the child's birth—promises that are linked with Old Testament predictions about the coming of a prophet who would be like Elijah and would, by the power of the Holy Spirit, announce the coming salvation of God. Zechariah, however, initially responds to this with doubt rather than faith; he is then rendered mute until the eventual birth of his promised son, John (1:18–25). By God's grace, and despite Zechariah's doubts, the child *is* born—the one who will come in the prophetic mold of Elijah to announce the coming of God's own Son: Jesus the Messiah.

Read Luke 1:1–25.

GETTING STARTED

1. What kinds of questions or critiques have you heard concerning the historicity of biblical accounts and the accuracy of Scripture? Which of these questions seem to be legitimate? How might others of these critiques, however, simply be serving to mask a resistance, on the part of those who raise them, to confronting the Bible's claims?

   Jesus not SOG Prophet

2. What role have struggles with *doubt* played in your Christian journey? When you have experienced times of doubt, what has helped you to strengthen your faith in God and his Word?

   The evil in the World
   " News of the World

The Ultimate Salvation, pg. 23

When Gabriel appeared and started talking about the spirit and power of Elijah, about turning the hearts of fathers to their children, and about getting people ready for God, he was announcing the ultimate salvation. These promises were for the ministry of Zechariah's son, but they went beyond John the Baptist to proclaim the coming of the Christ.

OBSERVING THE TEXT

3. What strikes you about Luke's introduction to his gospel (1:1–4)? What does he seem to want his audience to know about his approach to writing it? What might have made his approach important for believers in the first century?

THE FACTS

4. List some of the observations you have about Zechariah the priest, whom we get to know in this passage (1:5–25). What evidence do you see of his faithfulness, godliness, and obedience? What evidence do you see of his struggle with doubt?

AWARENESS

Keeping Posture in Society

5. How would you describe the promises that Gabriel makes to Zechariah in 1:13–17 regarding the son God will give to him? What makes these promises exciting—and why do you think Zechariah initially finds them too good to be true?

HIS AGE   HIS FAITH
THE IDEA ALL ARE FLAWED
GOD HAS EXTRODINARY POWERS

UNDERSTANDING THE TEXT

6. Why has Luke written this gospel, and to whom is it addressed (1:1–4)? What is his stated aim regarding Theophilus—and presumably all his readers?

   THEOPHILUS
   FOR THE TRUTH

7. How should Luke's introduction to his gospel shape your reading and study of it? What conclusions should you draw about what Luke will include in the book—and about what he might choose to leave out of it?

8. What does Luke tell us about Zechariah and Elizabeth as he first introduces them to us (1:5–7)? What makes them examples of godly believers who are emerging from the time of the Old Testament?

The Good Historian, pg. 7

Luke was a good historian. He did not write some fanciful account of things that people wanted to believe about Jesus, but an accurate historical record of what Jesus actually did. Through the testimony of Luke and others, the things that Jesus accomplished are as well established as any fact of ancient history, and this provides a rational basis for our faith.

9. The angel Gabriel links the coming child, John the Baptist, to the prophet Elijah (1:17). What do they have in common? How else will Zechariah's son act on behalf of God's people, according to what Gabriel says in 1:13–17?

10. What might have been the cause of the doubt that Zechariah expresses at Gabriel's words (1:18)? How does God discipline Zechariah in response—and what might he be teaching him by doing so (1:19–20)?

11. How does this passage conclude—and what does its conclusion reveal about the gracious heart God has for Zechariah and Elizabeth as well as for his people, Israel (1:24–25)? What do we learn about God's plan as he prepares for this great moment in salvation history?

BIBLE CONNECTIONS

12. Read John's introduction to his own gospel (John 1:1–18). In what way is his introduction different from the introduction to Luke's gospel? What would you say is John's main *emphasis* as he introduces Jesus— and then John the Baptist—to his readers?

13. The final words of the Old Testament—which were followed by four hundred years without any new revelation from God—come to us in Malachi 4:5–6. Read those verses now. What emotions would this prophecy have stirred up in the hearts of God's faithful people? In what clear ways do you see Gabriel's words to Zechariah echoing these verses?

THEOLOGY CONNECTIONS

14. One of the early heresies that plagued the church of the first century was *Gnosticism*—a system of belief that deplored the physical world as being evil while pursuing a higher form of saving knowledge (which could be attained regardless of how one sinned with one's physical body). In what way does Luke's historical, fact-based approach to telling the story of Jesus indicate that such a theory is mistaken? Why is it so important to believe that Jesus Christ came to earth in the *flesh*—that he lived as one who is fully God and fully human?

15. The Westminster Confession of Faith affirms that a Christian "believes to be true whatsoever is revealed in the Word, for the authority of God himself speaking therein" (14.2). What aspects of this standard does Zechariah at first fail to meet? Why is belief in God's Word a good indication of true, saving faith?

APPLYING THE TEXT

16. How can Luke's approach to writing this gospel serve to strengthen your faith in God and your confidence in the historicity of the Bible's accounts?

17. When we take Gabriel's words about John the Baptist seriously—and take the salvation of God, to which John will point, seriously as well—how will this shape our understanding of, and response to, the coming of Jesus Christ? In what way does this passage help your appreciation for the gospel to grow?

18. How can Zechariah's temporary lack of faith in God's Word serve as a negative example that drives you to have a deeper trust in all that God promises to you? Which of the promises God has made to you in Christ are you most prone to doubt—and why?

Taking God at His Word, pg. 27

This is what God always wants from us: faith. He wants us to take him at his word. So whatever God says, believe it! He has said that Jesus died and rose again, so believe in the crucifixion and the resurrection. He has said that he will forgive anyone who comes to him trusting in Jesus; so if you are a sinner, believe in Jesus and know that your sins are forgiven.

PRAYER PROMPT

As you come to the end of your first study within the gospel of Luke, begin your prayer by thanking God for the fact that he has acted in history—at real times and in real places—for the eternal good of sinful people in need. Praise him for Luke's "orderly" account, which focuses on the facts of what God's Son did and said in both time and space. Finally, pray that God would give you both an ever-deepening faith in his Word and his promises as well as the eternal hope of life and forgiveness that is yours through your faith in his Son, Jesus Christ the Messiah.

LESSON 2

MARY'S SONG

Luke 1:26–80

THE BIG PICTURE

Luke has begun his gospel by emphasizing the great anticipation that surrounded the imminent birth of the Messiah. Gabriel's prophetic words to Zechariah about his coming son, John the Baptist, describe him as the prophet who will be like Elijah and will prepare the hearts of God's people for the great day of salvation. The stage has been set for Jesus, the Christ, to come.

While the main focus of this lesson will be the rich and beautiful song that Mary sings when she meets with Elizabeth, we should also talk about the events that lead up to her praise-filled "Magnificat." The angel Gabriel has visited the young Mary and has told her that the Holy Spirit will miraculously enable her to conceive a child, who will be Jesus the Savior (1:26–38). Mary responds in faith and submits to the sure Word of God—in contrast with Zechariah the priest. Next, she travels to meet her relative Elizabeth, who by this point is pregnant with the child who will become John the Baptist (1:39–45). Elizabeth's unborn son "leaps" in her womb, which leads her to exclaim to Mary that her "Lord" dwells within Mary's womb. Mary responds to Elizabeth's words of faith with a song of praise (1:46–56).

The song itself is full of wonder and highlights Mary's faithful awareness of the promises God made to his people throughout the Old Testament. Mary speaks of how she has been "blessed" to bear the Messiah in her womb (v. 48). She delights in the great reversals that the birth of this child will bring about—that through him, God will tear down the proud and mighty and will exalt the estate of the poor and humble (vv. 51–52). Mary knows that her son, Jesus, will be the fulfillment of God's promises to his people Israel—which began even in the promises of blessing to Abraham (vv. 54–55). This first chapter of Luke's gospel concludes with the birth of John the Baptist, after which Zechariah regains his ability to speak (1:57–66). He responds to the birth of his son by giving a prophetic exclamation, in which he praises the God who keeps his promises and who visits his people with salvation (1:67–80).

Read Luke 1:26–80.

GETTING STARTED

1. When have you witnessed—and perhaps been disheartened by—a type of Christianity that seems *joyless*? Why is it such a sad and ironic contradiction for Christian faith and discipleship to lack joy?

   Congress, Sunday Morning Christians

2. What is your impression of people who keep their promises—who always follow through on what they say they will do? In what ways have people whom you can trust, and who always keep their word, personally benefitted you?

   Hunt, Palle

Covenant Connection, pg. 42

John was the greatest prophet of the old covenant—the one called to announce the coming of the Christ. Jesus *was* the Christ, the Lord of the new covenant. So when Mary met Elizabeth, the covenants connected. Both sons were joined under one roof, and like the electrical contact between two power stations, the results were explosive. There was a spontaneous outburst of exultant joy, as the old covenant greeted the new.

OBSERVING THE TEXT

3. What surprises you about the meeting that takes place between Mary and Elizabeth in Luke 1:39–45? What event takes place during their meeting that serves as a sign of God's supernatural work—and how does that event further signify what is to come?

   Leap for joy —

4. As you read through the song of praise that Mary offers to God, what initially strikes you about her attitude and tone throughout it (1:46–56)? What parts of the song reveal her humility? What specific attributes and actions of God does she consider praiseworthy?

   foresight to generat come
   Praise to god
   Resulting Kingdom

5. How does this passage shape your understanding of the significance of the coming of Jesus Christ, God's Son, into the world? What will the Messiah accomplish, according to the promises contained in Mary's song? What excites you about these promises? What makes you nervous about them?

   Mighty Deeds
   response to Ruler
   poor → Rich

UNDERSTANDING THE TEXT

6. What do you notice about the promises that Gabriel makes to Mary in 1:26–38 regarding the child she will bear? What do we learn about the identity of her child? How does Mary respond to what Gabriel tells her—and what shows that her response arises not from doubt but from faith in God and his Word?

Will be great
Throne of David for ever now

7. What can we learn from John the Baptist's joyful response of leaping in his mother's womb when she meets the pregnant Mary? How does this moment prophetically anticipate the ministry that he will have?

leam for joy

8. What specific cause does Mary give for praising God as she begins her song (1:46–50)? How does she describe her position before God? In what way do her words indicate that she has rightly understood the identity of the child she will bear?

Humble

Recognize and Rejoice, pg. 43
The coming of Christ is a thing that makes a person leap for joy. This was true for John, and also for anyone who comes to faith in Christ. By the inward witness of the Holy Spirit we recognize that Jesus is the Son of God and our Savior from sin. When we recognize him, we rejoice in him, leaping for the joy of our salvation.

9. Mary mentions several reversals that the coming of the Messiah will cause to happen both to God's people and to the world (1:51–53). What are these reversals? What do they show us about Jesus's reign and the kind of kingdom that he will bring?

Brought Down Rulers
Lifted the Humble
Hungre

10. How does Mary connect her coming pregnancy to the promises God has made to his people in the past (1:54–55)? Which of the promises that he made to Abraham might she have in mind (see Genesis 12, for example)?

Remember to be Merciful
Seed

11. Look through Mary's song of praise again. What Old Testament themes, references, and images do you notice? What do these things indicate about Mary's knowledge of God's Word—and about her attitude regarding the way God will fulfill his promises to his people through his coming Messiah?

Bless   *mighty Deeds*

BIBLE CONNECTIONS

12. Mary concludes her song by mentioning Abraham—the father of the Jewish people. Read Genesis 12:1–3, which records the initial call

and promises that God issued to Abraham. What connection is Mary drawing between the birth of the Messiah and those promises that God made so long ago?

Greatness, blessing

13. Many biblical scholars have highlighted the emphasis that Luke places throughout his gospel on Jesus's ministry to the poor. Look ahead for a moment to Luke 4:18–19. What text does Jesus read as he introduces his public ministry? What might have led him to choose this text—and what connection does it have with some of the themes we see in Mary's song?

Blind, to see

Poor hel

Hunger

THEOLOGY CONNECTIONS

14. While it is not the main theme of the passage we are studying, we do see God's regard for the unborn being made beautifully evident as he enables the unborn baby John to respond with joy and worship to the unborn Jesus Christ! In what way should seeing this shape our understanding of children within the womb—and of what we should do in response?

innocent guiloty

15. The theme of God's exaltation of the humble is evident throughout Mary's song of praise, as we have noted. Answer 27 of the Westminster Shorter Catechism notes that Jesus himself endured "humiliation" on earth, "being born . . . in a low condition, made under the law,

undergoing the miseries of this life, the wrath of God, and the cursed death of the cross." How does the direction of Jesus's life—from humiliation to exaltation—shape the lives of those who put their faith in him?

Shared life experience

APPLYING THE TEXT

16. What does the description of how the unborn John leaped for joy teach you about the right way to respond to the gospel of Jesus Christ? In what ways does this passage lead you to pray and to pursue a deeper joy in your Savior?

— peace and Happiness content not
— Joy — to be a christian

17. Mary responds to the almost unbelievable promise she receives from Gabriel with words of faith, hope, and praise to God. How can you model *your* response to the promises of God's Word on hers? And how can you imitate her faith and worship as you respond to what God has done for you in Christ?

Be thankful

The Lowly and the Lofty, pg. 52

This is the way God operates: the humble are shown mercy, while the proud receive justice. The lowly are lifted and the lofty are brought low. . . . The kingdoms of this world are temporary and transitory. God will not rest until Christ alone is Lord, and then he will see to it that justice is done, putting all wrongs to right.

18. Mary's words about the reversals that will happen as a result of Christ's coming and reign help us to gain a better perspective on the world powers of our day. In what ways could you allow this passage to shape your perspective on earthly power, pride, and might?

Rich Sloan   Jamie
Onin-py
Delores
Ron Scott
Ben

PRAYER PROMPT

As you close this lesson, begin your prayer by examining your response to Jesus Christ—to his coming, his grace, his salvation, and his return in judgment and power that is to come. Does your heart respond to him with joy? Pray that God would make your heart "leap" with faith, love, and worship for your Savior. Then ask him to continue to humble your heart as you look to Jesus in faith. Thank him that, in Christ, he exalts "those of humble estate" who will repent of sin and look to Christ alone as their Savior and King.

LESSON 3

THE BIRTH OF JESUS

Luke 2:1–38

THE BIG PICTURE

Luke has set the stage for the birth of Jesus Christ, the Messiah. John the Baptist, his forerunner, has been promised; he will come in the spirit of Elijah to announce the arrival of the Messiah. The angel Gabriel has promised further great things to Mary concerning the child she will bear with the help of the Holy Spirit; Mary responds to this with praise and worship and by wondering at her promise-keeping God. Now the time for Jesus's birth has come.

Luke emphasizes the humble nature of this birth: born in Bethlehem, the young Messiah is wrapped in swaddling cloths and laid in a manger (2:1–7). Staying true to his focus on the poor, the humble, and the outcast, Luke then records the first angelic announcement of Jesus's birth being given to shepherds in the fields at night (2:8–20). The sky is illuminated by a "multitude of the heavenly host," who sing praises to God and rejoice over the birth of the Messiah (vv. 13–14). These shepherds become the first worshipers to rush to the manger in order to see Jesus and to glorify and praise God for visiting his people (vv. 16, 20).

The final section of this passage describes Jesus's presentation in the temple, where his parents encounter two faithful saints, Simeon and Anna, who have been eagerly awaiting God's Messiah (2:21–38). Simeon, a righteous man to whom God has promised a glimpse of his Messiah, holds the baby Jesus in his arms and praises him as he speaks words of prophecy about his life and ministry (vv. 22–35). Anna, a widowed prophetess whose life is consumed by the worship of God, sees Jesus and immediately begins to spread the good news of God's coming salvation (vv. 36–38).

Read Luke 2:1–38.

GETTING STARTED

1. What tend to be indications in your culture of power, strength, and influence? How can our cultural ideas regarding power and influence contribute to unhealthy expectations about the earthly results of following Jesus?

   Cars Vacation Trips House

   Follow wrong God

2. Why do Christians sometimes lose their excitement about the gospel and their enthusiasm about the grace that God offers through Jesus Christ? What have you done, in the past, when you've struggled in your Christian walk with having joy and motivation?

   Humaness, Thinking must be More

   Get used to, Same all

   Does God get old?

God Is for Sinners, pg. 77

We tend to think that God is for the good people, when in fact he is for needy sinners who are desperate for grace. . . . Who better to exalt than lowly shepherds? We do not even know their names! If God had grace for them, he has grace for any poor sinner who will come to Jesus in faith.

OBSERVING THE TEXT

3. What initial observations do you have about Luke's account of the birth of Jesus Christ (2:1–7)? What does Luke emphasize about the circumstances that surrounded this birth?

Not overwhelming
the visitors /shepherds

4. How would you describe the demeanor and attitude that the shepherds in this passage display (2:8–20)? What do you know (or what can you assume) about the reputation, lifestyle, and place in society that characterized shepherds in the first century?

Overjoyed
Not Respful

5. What does Luke emphasize as he records how Simeon and Anna meet the baby Jesus in the temple? What does this serve to teach us about the expectations of God's people as well as about how God has kept his promises to Israel through the birth of Jesus?

Response, awaiting the Savior, all
in closue

UNDERSTANDING THE TEXT

6. What indication does the beginning of this passage give that Jesus's earthly parents are at the mercy of Caesar (2:1–5)? What do you think Caesar's purpose is behind the registration he decrees, and in what way

might Luke be subtly contrasting his rule with the rule of the true King who is about to be born?

Return Home Base – Differ Worlds
Count of People

7. What markers of humility and poverty does Luke's brief description of Jesus's birth contain (2:6–7)? How do these verses foreshadow the kind of earthly life and purpose that the Messiah will have?

Shepherds
Stable   with the needy
Clothing Everyday people

8. What is the main point of the message that the angel gives to the shepherds in the field (2:8–12)? What would have made this message such good news to Jews who had been waiting for a long time for the coming of the Christ?

Salvation, Savior

9. Note what the shepherds say to one another, as well as what they go on to do, after hearing the words of the angelic messengers (2:15–20). What do they seem to believe and accept about the birth of the child? How do they ultimately respond to the things they have seen and heard—and what is the reaction of people who hear them?

lets go see, Star

Glorifying

A Great Mystery, pg. 71

Everything we know about the birth of Jesus points to obscurity, indignity, pain, and rejection. One of the great mysteries of our universe is that when God the Son became a man he spent his first night in a barn.

10. After Jesus is circumcised and formally named (2:21), Mary and Joseph meet Simeon in the temple. How does Luke describe Simeon as he introduces him to his readers (2:25–27)? What significance does Simeon attach to Jesus's birth (2:28–32)? What does he prophesy to Mary concerning Jesus (2:34–35)?

Devout true Believer

to see god

Warning

11. What does Luke tell us about Anna's life and character (2:36–37)? In what way does she respond to the birth of Jesus (2:38)? How do the ways in which both she and Simeon react to seeing the infant Jesus remind us of the eternal significance of the coming of God's Son?

Devout, Constant Worship

BIBLE CONNECTIONS

12. Read Micah 5:1–2, which declares that the Messiah from God will be born in Bethlehem. What leads to Jesus's being born in Bethlehem, according to Luke's narrative, and how does this demonstrate God's sovereignty over the world and its rulers?

Roman Demand, Prophecy

13. Simeon's words about Jesus being a light for revelation to the Gentiles may be a reference to Isaiah 42:6. Begin with verse 1 of Isaiah 42, for

context, and read through to verse 6. How might these verses have shaped Simeon's expectation regarding what God would do through the Messiah who was to come?

Salvation
Questions

THEOLOGY CONNECTIONS

14. Throughout the early centuries of the church, many theological battles took place over how to rightly understand the divinity and humanity of Jesus Christ. Orthodox formulations of his humanity and divinity, such as the "Chalcedonian Definition," won the day; they explained that Jesus Christ is fully God and fully human—inseparably and without confusion. What details from the passage that we are studying demonstrate the full *humanity* of Jesus? What indications do they contain of his full *divinity*?

Birth,
Angels   foresight

15. Answer 22 of the Westminster Shorter Catechism summarizes Jesus's birth and incarnation with these words: "Christ, the Son of God, became man by taking to himself a true body, and a reasonable soul, being conceived by the power of the Holy Ghost, in the womb of the Virgin Mary, and born of her, yet without sin." We have seen Luke describing the true human birth of Jesus. Why is it so important to remember that Jesus was conceived by the Holy Spirit? What does this imply about Jesus regarding the topic of sin?

from God, By God
Not Human Birth/ Conception

APPLYING THE TEXT

16. What does his humble and lowly birth teach you about your Savior? How should this shape your expectations for the life that followers of Jesus live in this world, as well as for the path of discipleship?

Understanding our World
tests
Worries

17. How can the shepherds' response to the birth of Jesus guide your own response to your Savior? In what way do they model proper worship, praise, and humility? Why do you sometimes fail to respond to Jesus as they did? What changes could you make to your worship habits to make them more like theirs?

18. Simeon's words in 2:34, about how Jesus would cause the "rising" and "fall" of many, demand a response to the message of the gospel. How can his words motivate you to evangelize more boldly and courageously?

The Great Divide, pg. 97
What is your response to Jesus? Are you for him or against him? Will you rise or will you fall? This is the great question of life and death, because what God will do with us for all eternity depends on what we do with Jesus right now. He is the Great Divide.

PRAYER PROMPT

As you close your study of this beautiful passage, begin praying by praising God, with awe and wonder, that Jesus came to earth in such poverty, humility, and obscurity. Pray that you may be able to worshipfully bow before the Savior and King, who invites you to follow in the way of the cross—which is the path of humility. Ask God to give you a heart that rejoices at the hope of the gospel, as the shepherds did—and that praises the Savior God, as Simeon and Anna did!

LESSON 4

THE BOY JESUS

Luke 2:39–3:38

THE BIG PICTURE

As you saw in the previous lesson, Luke's description of the birth of Jesus is rich with theology and teaches us about God's promises to his people. Jesus is born in poverty and humility, which foreshadows his humble death on the cross. His birth, though, is accompanied by angelic worship as well as the praises of faithful saints who have long awaited the Messiah's coming. God's Son—the Savior and King—has come. He is born in humility but comes to accomplish all the saving purposes God has promised for his people.

The account you will study for this next lesson is unique to Luke; none of the other gospel writers include this incident. Luke gives us a glimpse into the boyhood Jesus spent under the care of his earthly parents, Joseph and Mary. This glimpse is bookended by verses in which Luke describes the "favor" of God that is on Jesus's life as he grows up in Nazareth (2:39–40, 52). Even before Jesus is revealed publicly as the Messiah, he experiences God the Father's presence, blessing, and approval throughout his earthly life.

Bracketed by these two summary statements is the one account we have of Jesus from between his birth and his adulthood: the story of the trip he takes with his parents to the temple in Jerusalem as a twelve-year-old boy (2:41–51). After inadvertently leaving him behind in Jerusalem, his parents return to find Jesus in the temple with the religious leaders, where he is talking with them and asking and answering questions (vv.

46–47). Jesus identifies the temple as the house of his "Father," which causes Mary to treasure and ponder his identity and purpose (vv. 49, 51). Luke highlights this one account from Jesus's boyhood in order to demonstrate that he is the Messiah and display his perfect submission to the will of his Father—the God of Israel.

We will not cover Luke 3 specifically in this lesson. Please read through that chapter as well, however—it covers the ministry of John the Baptist and includes his baptism of Jesus in the Jordan River (3:1-22). It then presents us with Jesus's genealogy, which moves backward from Joseph all the way to Adam (3:23-38).

Read Luke 2:39–3:38.

GETTING STARTED

1. What do you find challenging to understand about the incarnation of the second person of the Trinity? Have you ever wondered about the early years Jesus spent as a toddler, child, and teenager? What were you curious about?

Rebirth 12yr Old

Playmate, games

A Significant Story, pg. 102
Of all the things that Jesus said and did during his first thirty years, this is the only incident recorded in the Bible. Therefore, it must have special significance. What does this story tell us about Jesus? . . . What can we discover about his saving mission on earth? In this passage we see Jesus growing in stature, growing in wisdom, and learning obedience to his Father in heaven.

2. Why is it often so difficult for us to submit to authority? What sins tend to emerge in our hearts when we are called to submit to leaders, parents, or spiritual authorities with whom we do not always agree?

OBSERVING THE TEXT

3. What key words and ideas does Luke repeat, at the beginning and the end of this passage, as he summarizes Jesus's growth, development, and maturity (2:39–40, 52)? What does he seem to be emphasizing for his readers?

Wisdom Stature

4. How would you describe the boy Jesus who is portrayed throughout this passage? What about his words and actions surprises those around him? What makes him obviously different from other twelve-year-old boys of his day?

Obedient, obeying, Attentive
Maturity

5. What effect does this episode have on Mary . . . and what things might she have treasured up and pondered, regarding her son (2:51)?

His presence, and Maturity, honesty
Beliefs

UNDERSTANDING THE TEXT

6. How does Luke describe the way Jesus grew once he and his family returned to Nazareth (2:39–40)? This summary is echoed at the conclusion of this passage—what additional detail is included when it is (2:52)?

   Wisdom Stature,
   favor w God

7. Why is it important for Christians to remember that Jesus was truly both human and divine, throughout his entire life? What is mysterious about the fact that Jesus is both fully human and fully God? What foundational truths does Luke want us to keep in mind as we consider Jesus's formative years?

   Foresight, Ability to be in the time
   and know the future

8. What is Jesus doing in the temple when his parents discover him there—and what causes those who are around him to be so amazed (2:46–47)? What might Luke be seeking to communicate through this story about the kinds of questions Jesus was asking and the depth of his engagement with the Word of God?

   Communicat in

   Past
   Present
   Future
   All Realms

God in Three Persons, pg. 110–11

Here we are drawn into mysteries of the triune being of God. We have already pondered the mystery of the incarnation, that the divine Son of God had a human nature in every sense of the word. Here we are reminded that the one true God exists in three persons—Father, Son, and Holy Spirit. As the incarnate Son, Jesus knew God as Father even when he was a boy.

9. Note the response Jesus gives to Mary when she questions his decision to stay in Jerusalem (2:48–49). What does this show us about Jesus's awareness of his own identity and of the intimate relationship he has with the God of Israel? Why might it be that his parents don't fully understand his answer (2:50)?

Father, Have Maturity, Dismiss

10. What do we learn from the fact that Jesus submitted to his parents upon his return to Nazareth with them (2:51)? In what way is he obeying the commands of his heavenly Father, as well, by doing this?

Humans, Faithful Son, (People)

11. Luke tells us that Mary "treasured" these things in her heart (2:51). What kinds of questions might these events have also raised for both Mary and Joseph?

awe & Wonder

BIBLE CONNECTIONS

12. Read John 6:35–40, and note especially the way that Jesus connects his saving work to the will of the Father. How do we see Jesus's submission to the will of the Father being evidenced in this passage from Luke? Why is his submission to the Father good news for sinners who need salvation, according to these verses from John 6?

Eternal life —

13. Hebrews 2:17 tells us that Jesus was made like human beings "in every respect," so that he would be able to help us when we are tempted. How does our passage from Luke 2 further affirm and demonstrate the fact that Jesus Christ underwent the full human experience as a man? Why should this help to encourage you when you pray to God in the midst of weakness, frustration, or temptation?

THEOLOGY CONNECTIONS

14. The Westminster divines explain the doctrine of the Trinity with simplicity and clarity, noting that in the "unity" of the Godhead there are three persons "of one substance, power and eternity" (WCF 2.3). How do we see this doctrine being evidenced and developed within the passage we have been studying? What different roles of the persons of the Godhead does it demonstrate, and in what way does it indicate their fundamental unity of purpose?

15. This passage clearly demonstrates the submission of God the Son to God the Father—as do other places in Scripture (such as John 6:35–40). It is important to remember that Jesus's submission to the Father's will for the purpose of redemption does not imply any difference in their divinity: the Son is God; the Father is God; the Spirit is God. Why is it so important to our theology for us to maintain that a difference in roles does not imply a difference in value or identity?

APPLYING THE TEXT

16. In what way does this passage make you more amazed by Jesus—and more convinced of his identity as God's Son and our perfect Messiah?

17. How can Christ's submission to his earthly parents and his heavenly Father serve as an example for us as we interact with human authority and God's authority? In what area is God calling you to be more submissive right now?

god goes

K = 21

may man

18. This passage reminds us that Jesus remained truly human as he grew and developed. What encouragement should you take from the fact that your Lord and Savior has lived a real human life?

Perfect Submission, pg. 113

Jesus submitted to God's will for our salvation. God the Son became a human being, with a mind and a body like ours. He grew through the stages of life, facing all the struggles that we face. . . . He submitted to God's will, even to the point of obeying his parents. Jesus did all this so that he could live a perfect life and then offer himself as the perfect sacrifice for our sins.

PRAYER PROMPT

As you conclude your study of this passage, begin praying by thanking God the Father for the "favor" that this passage tells us he placed on the life of Jesus Christ—God the Son. Praise him that, because of the perfect obedience and submission of Jesus Christ, sinners can be saved through his work on the cross and the gift of his righteousness! Then ask God for a humble heart that, after the pattern of your Savior, submits to him—and to those who are in authority in your life—as you live for the glory of Jesus Christ.

LESSON 5

JESUS'S PREPARATION

Luke 4:1–13

THE BIG PICTURE

As you saw in the previous lesson, Jesus was conscious of the special relationship that God had with him, as his Father, even from a young age. He grew up in favor with God and man, and submitted to his earthly parents during his childhood and teenage years, as he waited for the Father's timing before launching his public ministry. In Luke 4:1–13, you will see him undergoing his intense period of ministry preparation in the wilderness, when the devil directly tempts him in multiple ways.

In the wilderness, Jesus faces what very few human beings have to face: a direct, powerful onslaught from Satan himself as he tempts him to sin. Satan begins by provoking Jesus, who has been fasting for forty days, to use his divine power to turn stones into bread (4:1–3). Jesus resists the devil and uses Scripture to point to the greater source of sustenance that God's Word provides (4:4). Next, Satan tempts Jesus to grasp for the authority and glory of the world, which he offers to turn over to Jesus in exchange for his worship (4:5–7). Jesus turns to the Word of God again and invokes its call to worship the Lord God alone (4:8). Finally, the devil tempts Jesus to abuse his divine power by throwing himself from the pinnacle of the temple in Jerusalem; Jesus, however, refuses to put God the Father to the test, which is again in accordance with Scripture (4:9–12).

The devil ultimately departs from Jesus after failing to lure the Son of God into sin (4:13). Jesus has withstood this time of testing in the wilderness and has held to God's Word in perfect faith and obedience. He has succeeded where God's people have failed—and has demonstrated perfect righteousness and perfect obedience to the Father.

Read Luke 4:1–13.

GETTING STARTED

1. How do you tend to deal with being tempted to sin—whether in the area of your speech, your actions, your viewing habits, or your thoughts? What strategies have been effective for helping you to resist in the past—and what strategies have been ineffective?

2. What causes us to forget the fact that Jesus Christ was fully human? What dangers result from our emphasizing his *divinity* to the exclusion of his *humanity*?

Tested and Triumphant, pg. 161

Three diabolical temptations, met by three biblical responses—and when it was all over, Satan had to leave in disgrace. . . . Their struggle would not be over until they battled to the death. But for the time being, Jesus had triumphed, resisting and refusing every temptation. What Satan intended as a temptation actually turned out to be a test or trial that proved the saving innocence of Jesus.

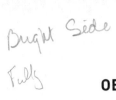
Bright Side
Fully

OBSERVING THE TEXT

3. What roles do God the Father and God the Holy Spirit play in the actions Jesus takes in this passage? How does the narrative make it clear that Jesus (God the Son) is walking in unified step with the Father and the Spirit?

4. What makes the devil's strategies so pernicious, dangerous, and cunning? What do the temptations that he brings before Jesus have in common with the temptations that every human being faces?

5. What approach does Jesus take as he responds to the devil's temptation? What pattern do we see emerging throughout the passage?

UNDERSTANDING THE TEXT

6. What does Luke say to make it clear that Jesus's time in the wilderness—which includes his temptation by the devil—has been ordained by God and intended as part of his preparation for ministry (4:1–2)? Why is it important for us to understand this experience as being ordained by God the Father and prompted by the Spirit?

7. What would have made the devil's first temptation, in 4:3 (to turn stone into bread), intense and powerful? How does Jesus resist this temptation—and what truth does he embrace as he rejects the devil's prompting (4:4)?

8. What promise does the devil make to Jesus as he tempts him for a second time—and what does he require from him in return for this promised gift (4:5–7)? On what does Jesus found the response he gives to the devil—and what command from God's Word does he quote to him (4:8)?

9. Note the final temptation that Satan puts before Jesus, in 4:9–11. In what way does this temptation target Jesus's identity as the Messiah and his relationship to God the Father? Why might this seem like a powerful temptation from the devil's perspective? What does he do to add force to this third temptation?

The Wilderness Test, pg. 152

Jesus and Satan squared off in the wilderness. This takes us back to the place where the Israelites wandered, not for forty days, but for forty years. Just as the children of Israel were tested, so also Jesus—the true Israel—would be tested in the wilderness. There he would do what God's people had failed to do: live in grateful obedience to God.

10. What is powerful about Jesus's response to this final temptation (4:12)? How could his simple answer serve to guide us regarding our own responses to temptation and trial?

11. In what way do we see the perfect righteousness and obedience of Jesus the Son being displayed throughout this passage? What is Luke showing his readers—and why is it so important for us to understand the character of Jesus as he prepares for his public ministry, teaching, and ultimately crucifixion?

BIBLE CONNECTIONS

12. Read Genesis 3:1–7—the account of Adam and Eve sinning in the garden of Eden after being tempted by Satan. What similarities do you see between this passage and the one from Luke we have been studying? What is cunning about the approach that Satan takes with Adam and Eve? How is their response to him massively different from Jesus's?

13. Hebrews 3:15–19 describes the Israelites' years of wandering in the wilderness, their hardened hearts, and their sin against God. Read that passage now. How does this account from Luke 4 serve as a kind of

revisiting of those forty years in the wilderness—and how do we see Jesus proving, in it, that he is the true, perfect, righteous Israel of God?

THEOLOGY CONNECTIONS

14. Answer 39 of the Westminster Larger Catechism affirms how important it was that Jesus our Mediator became fully human in order to be able to "perform obedience to the law, suffer and make intercession for us in our nature, [and] have a fellow-feeling of our infirmities." How does Luke 4:1–13 show us that Jesus Christ, because of his humanity, has an understanding of our weakness—what the catechism calls our "infirmities"? Why is this encouraging to followers of Jesus, like us, who struggle with pain, weakness, and temptation?

15. Reformed theology speaks of the *passive righteousness* of Christ, which refers to his death on the cross—to which he submitted in the place of God's sinful people. It also speaks of the *active righteousness* of Christ, which refers to the way that he perfectly fulfilled the law of God on behalf of God's people by living the perfect human life in obedience to the Father. What makes Luke 4 a key passage in the Bible for understanding the *active righteousness* of Jesus Christ?

APPLYING THE TEXT

16. What do you learn from Luke 4 about the *kinds* of temptation that the devil—or his servants—may place in your path as you seek to follow Jesus? How can this passage serve to make you more aware of temptations you experience to follow ways of thinking, acting, or believing?

17. How should the example that Jesus sets in this passage shape your own struggle against sin and temptation? What role should the Word of God play in your fight against sin? What can you do to rely more closely on the Spirit for help during the struggle?

18. Ultimately, how does this passage lead you to respond to Jesus Christ—your perfect substitute who has walked righteously in your place? Why is it such good news for *you* that Jesus overcame temptation in the wilderness?

Victory Gained, pg. 163

Our victory comes through the victory of Jesus Christ. Jesus did what he did against the devil so that he could gain us victory in our struggle against sin. If we had to face the devil without the saving work of Jesus Christ and without the gracious help of his Spirit, we wouldn't last more than a millisecond. But we do not face temptation alone.

PRAYER PROMPT

As you close your study of this passage, begin praying by praising God for his Son, Jesus—the perfect substitute, the true Israel, and the one who fulfilled all righteousness in your place. He lived the life that you could not live and died the death that you deserved to die. Praise him who lived—and died—in your place! Then ask God to strengthen you against sin and temptation as you seek to follow the footsteps of your Savior. Thank him for his Word and for the Spirit's presence as you resist sin and obey him.

LESSON 6

JESUS THE PREACHER

Luke 4:14–44

THE BIG PICTURE

Upon emerging from the wilderness after having triumphed over Satan's temptation, Jesus formally begins his public ministry. The remainder of Luke 4 presents Jesus as the *preacher* from God—a preacher who supports his message with authoritative acts of exorcism and healing. Even though he does so, however, the Messiah will not be accepted by everyone—not even in the town where he grew up.

Jesus returns to his hometown of Nazareth, visits the synagogue, and opens the scroll of the book of Isaiah to read a passage that describes for God's people the salvation and freedom that his Anointed One will bring (4:14–21). Jesus makes the bold assertion that his coming has fulfilled the expectation and hope of the prophet Isaiah. Ultimately, though, he is rejected by many in his own hometown who question both his identity and his authority (4:22–30). When he responds to their wonder and confusion about him by alluding to God's historic welcome of people outside the community of Israel, he is driven out of town by angry crowds. Jesus then continues his public ministry by not only preaching with authority but also performing wonderful signs—such as exorcising demons with authority as well, along with healing all kinds of diseases—which illustrate his identity as both the Messiah and a divine authority from God (4:31–44). The passage concludes with Jesus quieting the demons whose cries identify him as the

Son of God and then continuing to preach in the synagogues of Judea as he calls men and women to repent and put their faith in him.

Read Luke 4:14–44.

GETTING STARTED

1. What objections to the claims of Jesus do your friends raise who do not believe in him? What is offensive about the Bible's message of salvation through Christ to people in your culture?

2. What problems could arise, in the life of a Christian, from focusing too much on earthly physical healing without considering the hope we have of eternity with Jesus and of our lives in the resurrection? What do the healings that Jesus performs in this passage tell us about his power and identity, as well as about the ultimate hope for eternal, physical healing that belongs to those who put their faith in him?

The First and Best Sermon, pg. 164
Of all the great sermons that have been preached since the beginning of the world, no one has ever preached a better sermon than the first one that Jesus preached in his hometown of Nazareth. It brings people to saving faith, gives them hope in all their troubles, and helps them see the glory of the Son of God. What could be better than to hear our Savior preach, and preach about himself?

OBSERVING THE TEXT

3. What makes Jesus's claims in the synagogue at Nazareth so startling? Why does the statement he makes after reading from Isaiah shock the people who are listening (4:16–22)?

4. What seems to have driven the angry rejection of Jesus by the people in Nazareth (4:23–30)? Why might his references to Old Testament Gentiles have made his opponents angry (vv. 25–27)?

5. In what ways does Luke emphasize Jesus's identity, power, and authority throughout 4:31–44? What *kinds* of authority does Jesus exert throughout these verses?

UNDERSTANDING THE TEXT

6. What do 4:14–15 tell you about the reputation Jesus is developing and about how the people are receiving the teaching he is performing in the synagogues?

7. Whom would faithful Jews have expected to fulfill the prophetic words that Jesus reads in the synagogue at Nazareth (4:18–19)? What stunning claim does Jesus make—and what does this teach us about his understanding of his identity and significance (4:20–21)?

8. While some people marvel at Jesus, others—specifically those in Nazareth—balk at his claim to authority (4:28–29). Why do you think the people in Nazareth reject him after having initially received him positively in 4:22? What does Jesus say about their rejection of him?

9. Note the angry violence that starts to be directed at Jesus at this early point in his public ministry (4:28–30). What does this foreshadow? How does his escape from the crowd, in verse 30, illustrate his divine authority and plan?

Fulfillment, pg. 169
Jesus was announcing the fulfillment of Isaiah's prophecy. The anointed one, the Messiah, the Christ had come. The Suffering Servant had arrived, bringing salvation. And with him came all the things that Isaiah promised would only come on the great day of God: good news for the poor, freedom for the captives, sight for the blind, and liberty for people under oppression.

10. Over what realm does Jesus exert his authority when he exorcises a demon in Capernaum (4:31–37)? Why is this significant? How does the demon demonstrate a deeper understanding of Jesus's identity than many from Jesus's own hometown do?

11. What does Jesus's ongoing healing ministry, which we see in 4:38–40, demonstrate about the attitude he takes toward people in conjunction with seeing them as complete persons—as physical and spiritual beings? How does Jesus view his preaching ministry—and why is this important for us to remember (4:41–44)?

BIBLE CONNECTIONS

12. Read John 5:37–40, which records the indignant response Jesus gives to the Jewish religious leaders who know the Old Testament Scriptures thoroughly and yet still reject him. What does Jesus tell them about the purpose of these Scriptures, their trajectory, and the way they have been fulfilled? How should his message to them shape the way we study the Old Testament as Christians today?

13. In response to the skepticism that he experiences from many people in Nazareth, Jesus references how God pursued Gentiles in the Old Testament during a time of rebellion and disobedience in Israel, and he specifically mentions Naaman (from 2 Kings 5) and the widow of Zarephath (from 1 Kings 17). Review those stories briefly. Why might Jesus be choosing to point back to these accounts at this particular moment?

THEOLOGY CONNECTIONS

14. Answer 24 of the Westminster Shorter Catechism explains that Jesus serves as God's ultimate prophet for his people: "Christ executes the office of a prophet, in revealing to us, by his word and Spirit, the will of God for our salvation." What makes Jesus's prophetic role especially evident in the passage we have been studying for this lesson?

15. In his well-known hymn "A Mighty Fortress," Martin Luther celebrates the authority that the name of Jesus has over even Satan himself: "One little word shall fell him!" How do Jesus's interactions with the demons in this passage demonstrate the utter helplessness of the kingdom of darkness against his power?

APPLYING THE TEXT

16. In what way ought this passage to increase your appreciation for Jesus Christ's work in the world—and in your life? How can its revelation of his authority drive you to worship, be awed by, and revere your Savior all the more?

17. What insight does this passage provide into the hearts and motivations of those who *reject* Jesus Christ? What about the message of the gospel might make them angry? What causes many people to doubt Jesus, and how can Christians address their doubts and criticisms?

18. What truths in this passage should inform the way in which you share the hope of the gospel of Jesus with others? What makes the message about Jesus such good news for a sinful and broken world?

Holistic Healing, pg. 196

In his healing work as our Great Physician, Jesus is concerned for the whole person—body and soul. . . . Sometimes we wish that God would just hurry up and heal us. If he doesn't, it is not because he doesn't love us, but because he is working a better plan. In the meantime, we need to trust him to do his total work in our lives.

PRAYER PROMPT

As you conclude your study of this passage that has portrayed Jesus as the authoritative preacher and healer, spend some time praising and thanking God for his Word of truth and for the eternal healing he has brought to your soul through your faith in Christ. Thank him for revealing the truth of the gospel to you through his Word. Thank him for the fact that you are spiritually healed—forgiven—and that you will one day be made perfect physically as well. Ask God for physical healing, now, for those who are suffering. Pray for the humility and grace to receive Jesus by faith—and to live by every word that your God has spoken!

LESSON 7

THE CALL OF THE DISCIPLES

Luke 5:1–6:16

THE BIG PICTURE

The key events of this lesson's passage are interwoven with healing miracles that Jesus performs. As is evident from the way it begins and ends, a major theme of the passage is Jesus's gathering of his twelve disciples—the men who will follow him closely and learn from him during his public ministry on earth. He calls this group of men from different backgrounds to follow him closely so that they can one day proclaim the good news about him to the world.

Simon (who is also known as Peter), James, and John are the first disciples to be chosen; Jesus calls them away from their fishing business, and they follow him immediately (5:1–11). Next comes Luke's record of Jesus healing a leper and a paralytic—as well as getting into a confrontation with the Pharisees, during the latter, regarding his authority to forgive people's sins (5:12–26). Jesus also calls Levi (also known as Matthew), who works as a tax collector for the Romans (5:27–32). Both the Pharisees and the scribes criticize Jesus and grumble angrily about his association with "sinners" such as Matthew and his friends (v. 30).

Before Luke gives a final list of the twelve disciples who are gathered by Jesus, he describes three events and interactions that illustrate the significance of the Messiah's coming and the way in which it fulfills prophecies—as well as the rejection he encounters from the Jewish religious leaders. First, Jesus explains to his disciples that his coming is a time for rejoicing and not

63

for fasting, because the salvation of God has arrived (5:33–39). Second, following yet another criticism from the Pharisees—this time regarding Sabbath restrictions—Jesus explains that the Son of Man (Jesus himself) is Lord over the Sabbath (6:1–5). Third, as he heals a man's withered hand on the Sabbath Day, Jesus again demonstrates his authority to do good— even on the Lord's Day (6:6–11). After this, Luke lists all the men whom the Son of Man has called to leave everything and follow him—God's true Messiah (6:12–16).

Read Luke 5:1–6:16.

GETTING STARTED

1. Do you think that many Christians today see their faith in Jesus as involving discipleship? Why or why not? In what other ways do Christians tend to think about their faith—or about the Christian religion?

   No Faith Journey

2. What comes into your mind when you hear the word *disciple*? Does that word carry a positive or negative connotation in your culture today? Explain.

   Over used

The Meaning of Discipleship, pg. 203
[Luke] wants to bring us to the point of making a decision for discipleship. As soon as we know for sure that Jesus is the Christ, we must follow him, which is what it means to be a disciple. A disciple follows Jesus and never turns back.

OBSERVING THE TEXT

3. What do you notice about the way Luke portrays the men whom Jesus calls to be his disciples—specifically in terms of the types and amounts of detail he provides for each one? Why do you think he goes into more detail about Peter, James, John, and Matthew than about the other disciples?

Main Character —

4. What common themes do you notice across the interactions Jesus has with the Pharisees, scribes, and religious leaders throughout this passage? How do these men consistently react to him? Why might this be the case?

They are threatend
Moses and Brothes

5. At what key points in this passage does Jesus reveal his identity and authority—and how? What makes the Messiah's coming good news for those who are sick, sinful, and needy?

Pharises
Rules

UNDERSTANDING THE TEXT

6. What does Jesus demonstrate in Luke 5:1–7 about his identity and power? What is Simon Peter's response to Jesus—and why (5:8–9)? How do Peter, James, and John ultimately respond to Jesus's invitation (5:10–11)?

7. Why do the Pharisees and scribes react negatively to what Jesus says to the paralytic (5:17–21)? What does Jesus seek to demonstrate by healing the paralyzed man—and why is this significant to an understanding of Jesus's purpose (5:22–25)? How do the people react to this healing (5:26)?

8. What makes the calling of Matthew—a tax collector—surprising (5:27–28)? How do the Pharisees and scribes react when Jesus identifies with tax collectors and "sinners"—and what lesson does Jesus give them about his purpose and coming (5:29–32)?

Don't want to lose Control
Special Status , More Special
Animal Farm

Faulty Reasoning, pg. 224
The scribes and Pharisees failed to recognize that Jesus Christ *is* God the eternal Son. This is why they accused him of blasphemy. By forgiving people's sins, Jesus was effectively claiming to be God. But he *wasn't* God, at least as far as they could see. . . . There was only one problem with their reasoning: Jesus really *is* God!

9. Note the response Jesus gives to the Pharisees and scribes' question about fasting—and the parable that follows it (5:33–39). What is he explaining to them about his identity and the good news of his coming?

Rejoice

10. Two confrontations between Jesus and the Pharisees precede Luke's final summary of the calling of the twelve disciples—and both confrontations erupt because of Sabbath Day law (6:1–11). What does Jesus demonstrate about his identity by comparing himself to King David and confirming the authority that he holds over the Sabbath (6:1–5)? What does he teach about God's ultimate purpose regarding the Sabbath Day (6:6–11)?

Who can forgive —

Prophesies

11. What have you already learned about Jesus's disciples before Luke lists their full number (6:12–16)? What additional details does Luke provide for us about these men when he names all twelve of them together?

BIBLE CONNECTIONS

12. Jesus references 1 Samuel 21:1–6 when the Pharisees confront his disciples for plucking heads of grain on the Sabbath. Read that passage

now. Why might Jesus have decided to invoke this passage during this interaction? What similarities is he suggesting between David's situation and his own coming as the Messiah to Israel?

13. In Revelation 21:14, upon being given a vision of the holy city of new Jerusalem, John writes that "the wall of the city had twelve foundations, and on them were the twelve names of the twelve apostles of the Lamb." In what way does the number twelve hark back to the Old Testament and the history of the work that God has done within the people of Israel? What does John's vision of the holy city of God tell us about the significance of these twelve disciples and of their work of witnessing to Jesus in the world—as well as about their foundational role in the beginning of the New Testament church?

THEOLOGY CONNECTIONS

14. The Westminster Confession of Faith instructs God's people to be, on the Lord's Day, "taken up, the whole time, in the public and private exercises of his worship, and in the duties of necessity and mercy" (21.8). In what way do these instructions reflect the attitude that Luke describes Jesus taking toward the Sabbath in this lesson's passage? What causes worship and "duties of necessity and mercy" to fit so well together on the Lord's Day?

15. As our Great High Priest, Jesus Christ "executes the office of a priest, in his once offering up of himself a sacrifice to satisfy divine justice, and reconcile us to God; and in making continual intercession for us" (WSC 25). How does this doctrinal statement help to explain why Jesus is able to insist that he has "authority" on earth to forgive sins (Luke 5:24)?

    Walk-the Walk
    Walk the talk

APPLYING THE TEXT

16. What encourages you about the kinds of men whom Jesus calls to be his disciples—namely, humble fishermen, political zealots, and tax-collecting "sinners"? How does this serve to remind you of your own sin, weakness, and need—as well as of the rich mercy and grace that God has shown to you in Christ?

17. Have you been guilty of reacting as the Pharisees did to aspects or implications of the gospel? Which ones? What could you do to engage "sinners" and spiritually broken people in a Christlike way as you invite them to know the love and grace of God?

18. How can you pattern your own discipleship after the way the disciples in this passage immediately pursue Jesus and obey his call? What steps could you take, this very week, to more actively and wholeheartedly move forward in your discipleship under Jesus?

PRAYER PROMPT

As you close your study of this rich passage from the gospel of Luke, begin your prayer by praising God for delighting to call sinners to himself, for saving them through the work of his Son, and for inviting them to follow Jesus, through the power of the Spirit, as his disciples. Then ask God to deepen your commitment to walking as a disciple of Jesus. Pray that he would work in your heart to make you open to welcoming sinners to the gracious Savior and to joyfully calling them to repentance and faith in the same Lord who has so richly welcomed you.

The Spirit Does the Real Work, pg. 257
Whether we are nobodies like the apostles when Jesus called them, or somebodies such as they became, we need to put our confidence in Christ alone, and not in ourselves, so that his Spirit can do the real work of our ministry.

LESSON 8

JESUS'S TEACHING

Luke 6:17–49

THE BIG PICTURE

Jesus has gathered the twelve disciples to himself—men from many different backgrounds, many of whom are humble and despised by the world. Now he will begin to *teach* them. What will the path of discipleship look like for those who follow the Messiah? What will the values and blessings of his kingdom be? How will the followers of Jesus relate to the world around them as they walk according to their Savior's example?

Jesus, the teacher, calls his disciples to embrace the upside-down values of his kingdom, which will unavoidably clash with the values and pursuits of a sinful world. For instance, God's blessing, according to Jesus, comes to the poor and the hungry—to those who weep and those who are persecuted for their faith in him (6:17–23). Conversely, the "woe" and judgment of God will come to those who are rich and full of food—who carelessly seek pleasure and receive the approval of the world around them (6:24–26). After pronouncing these words of blessing and woe, Jesus moves on to a striking and difficult command as he calls his disciples to love their enemies—even those who seek to persecute and cause violence to the people of God (6:27–36). The path of discipleship under Jesus will involve humility, as well—rather than embracing a judgmental attitude toward others, his disciples are called to identify the sin that is in their own lives (6:37–42). Ultimately, disciples of Jesus are called to build their lives on *his* words,

71

person, and example—for only through this pursuit will they bear good "fruit" for God's glory and the good of the world around them (6:43–49).

Read Luke 6:17–49.

GETTING STARTED

1. What would you say are the main things that people in your culture pursue? What are the typical markers of blessing and success in that culture?

   money
   FAME
   TRIPS

   Hungrier Ego
   the Bumper sticker

2. Why is it so difficult to love people who have terribly wronged you or hurt you? Even if you resist taking revenge against those who have done this, what kinds of thoughts, feelings, and temptations fill your heart in response to their hurtful actions or words?

   Dont want the pain
   And Ridicule

Unexpected, pg. 259

How can you tell that God is blessing you? The answer Jesus gives is totally unexpected. He takes the things that no one wants—poverty, hunger, sorrow, persecution—and says that they have his blessing. Then he takes the things that everyone wants—money, food, entertainment, popularity—and says that they will never satisfy.

OBSERVING THE TEXT

3. What do you notice from 6:17–19 about the context in which Jesus's teaching takes place? What is he doing before he begins teaching, and how is the crowd reacting to him? To whom does his teaching seem to be primarily directed (6:20)—and why is this significant?

those who are more possesive

4. What are some of the main contrasts that Jesus draws between those who are "blessed" and those who receive "woe" (6:20–26)? What might have made these words surprising to Jesus's disciples—as well as to people who read them today?

those is woe are blessed spiritually

5. How does 6:46–49 demonstrate that Jesus's teaching is grounded in his identity, authority, and power? Why is it not enough, then, for us to accept Jesus merely as a good teacher rather than as the Son of God and Savior of the world?

Hearers

UNDERSTANDING THE TEXT

6. Describe the crowd that Luke says has amassed to hear Jesus and receive healing from him (6:17–19). What do you notice about the people who gather around him? In what ways does Jesus demonstrate his compassion, and what signs does he give of his identity, authority, and power?

7. What surprising reversals do Jesus's promises regarding blessing involve (6:20–23)? What blessings does he say will come to those who endure great humility and suffering in this life? What reversals are in store for those who have treasured riches, pleasure, and popularity above all else in this life (6:24–26)?

— Heard Spirit -

8. What makes the commands that Jesus gives his disciples regarding their enemies so difficult and surprising (6:27–31)? How does he link these difficult commands to the character of God, and what does he say about the eternal blessing that awaits his disciples who follow these commands (6:32–36)? What ultimate example would Jesus go on to provide for his disciples of how to love one's enemies?

9. Why does Jesus command his disciples in 6:37–38 not to "judge" others—and what does he mean by saying so? How does he teach that his followers should deal with sin in their own lives and hearts (6:39–42)? In what way can this approach to dealing with it serve to guard them against judgmentalism and hypocrisy?

10. What makes Jesus's metaphor of the tree and its fruit, from 6:43–45, a helpful metaphor for his disciples as they seek to follow the teaching of their Savior and Lord? How can this picture help us to distinguish Jesus's teaching from mere moralism or legalism?

11. How do Jesus's pictures of the house "on the rock" and the house "without a foundation" serve as helpful summaries of his teaching (6:46–49)? What does it look like to build a life on the words of Jesus—and why does doing so require acceptance of his claims about his identity?

Unwanted Blessings, pg. 263

Most people say they want God to bless them, but how many people really want to live the kind of Christ-centered life that God has promised to bless? Most people do not want to be poor; they want to get rich. They do not want to go hungry; they want to get stuffed. They do not want to weep; they want to crack jokes. They do not want to get persecuted; they want to be popular.

BIBLE CONNECTIONS

12. Luke's record of Jesus's Sermon on the Plain corresponds to Matthew's record of Jesus's Sermon on the Mount—which is a longer version of the same teaching. Take a few minutes to glance through Matthew 5–7. What additional teaching from Jesus does Matthew include? As you bear in mind the themes of his gospel, explain why Luke might have chosen to focus on the specific teachings that he records in this chapter.

Ask seek Knock
give

13. Read Ecclesiastes 7:2, which declares that it is better to enter a house of "mourning" than a house of "feasting." How does this statement concur with what Jesus says in verses 21 and 25 of this passage from Luke? How can the practice of mourning in this life—over our sin and over the brokenness in the world—help to draw us closer to the heart of God and enable us to treasure Jesus more?

THEOLOGY CONNECTIONS

14. Jesus does not equate spiritual blessing with the size of one's bank account—whether that amount is high or even low (6:20, 24). There is a poverty of spirit that characterizes *all* Jesus's true disciples when they repent of sin and turn to him in faith as spiritually bankrupt sinners. Still, Jesus's teaching does not avoid the topic of possessions. Compared to very wealthy people, why might those who have fewer material possessions find it easier to treasure Christ? What temptations

and roadblocks do great material possessions introduce in the areas of humility and childlike faith?

15. J. C. Ryle describes the love that Jesus commands as being "unselfish, disinterested, and uninfluenced by any hope of return."[1] In what way does Jesus provide the ultimate example of this kind of love? Why must the cross of Jesus serve as our purest and best model for how to love people who appear undeserving?

APPLYING THE TEXT

16. Note that while 6:17–19 tells us that Jesus has been continuing to heal many people, his teaching in this passage is directed primarily to his disciples—to the men who are already following him (6:20). Why is this important for us to understand? What application of this teaching should we, as followers of Jesus, make to ourselves? Why must the path of discipleship always start with the saving grace that Jesus Christ offers to sinners?

---

1. J. C. Ryle, *Expository Thoughts on the Gospels: Luke* (1858; repr., Cambridge: James Clarke, 1976), 1:183, quoted in Philip Graham Ryken, *Luke*, vol. 1, *Chapters 1–12* (Phillipsburg, NJ: 2009), 277.

17. In what areas has this passage shown you that you desire worldly blessing rather than God's eternal blessing? What are some ways that you can more wholeheartedly embrace the values of Jesus's kingdom—and can root out your desire for worldly significance or glory?

18. What can you do to more intentionally love your "enemies" (6:27–28)? How must your response to those who mistreat you, insult you, or harm you be shaped by the cross of Christ?

PRAYER PROMPT

As you close your study of Jesus's teaching about the true and eternal blessings that await those who follow him, ask God to give you the strength, through his Spirit, to joyfully receive this teaching from your Savior and Lord. Pray to be able to pursue the values of Jesus's kingdom—not the kingdom of this world. Pray that you may desire God's blessing—not the temporal pleasure of sin. Finally, pray that God would enable you to love even your enemies, as you remember that Jesus your Savior died for you while you were still an enemy of God because of your sin.

Love at the Cross, pg. 277

This is where we learn to love our enemies: at the cross, where we were the enemies that Jesus died to forgive. Surely this is one of the reasons why Jesus gave us such a hard commandment. It is not a commandment that we could ever keep out of the strength of our own love. In order to keep it, we have to stay close to the cross, holding on to the love we know that Jesus showed us there.

LESSON 9

JESUS'S HEALING

Luke 7:1-35

THE BIG PICTURE

In the previous lesson, Jesus taught his disciples about the eternal values of his kingdom—values that are often upside-down, from the world's perspective, but that reflect the heart of a gracious, just, and loving God. In the passage for this lesson, you will see that Jesus bears witness to his eternal kingdom through *healing* as well as through teaching. The many powerful signs he performs demonstrate the authority and identity that belong to him as the Son of God and also give glimpses into the beauty of his eternal kingdom and perfect salvation.

The passage begins with a Roman centurion who sends word to Jesus about his sick servant, who is near death (7:1–10). Jesus begins to go to his house, only to encounter the centurion's surprising faith: he trusts that Jesus has the power and authority to merely *speak* from a distance in order to bring healing to his servant. As a result, Jesus holds this centurion up as a model of faith.

Luke next records that Jesus has deep compassion for a widow whose only son has just died and then raises the son to life—causing great amazement and wonder to spread throughout the people of the area (7:11–17). In the midst of this powerful healing ministry, John the Baptist sends messengers to Jesus to inquire about his identity (7:18–23). Jesus responds by pointing out the powerful signs and wonders that they have seen—signs and wonders that proclaim his identity and demand a response of faith in the

Messiah. The chapter concludes with Jesus explaining to his disciples the significance of John the Baptist's ministry (7:24–35). God's true people are called to respond in faith to the words of this great prophet and forerunner to the Christ—as well as to Jesus himself!

Read Luke 7:1–35.

GETTING STARTED

1. What challenges have you heard people raise regarding the reliability of Scripture or the divinity of Jesus Christ? What objections to these truths do you think are the most common—and why?

   Un Believing

   Thning Facth

2. How have you dealt with *doubt* in your walk with the Lord? In what way can occasional doubts and seasons of questioning be helpful for our growth in Christ, depending on how we deal with them?

   No Doubt

   Ends are assured

   Earth Temporary

Foreshadowing the Death of Death, pg. 322

The raising of the widow's son does point us to the death of death in the resurrection of Jesus Christ. It is one of the first hints in the Gospel that Jesus would rise from the dead. In compassion for our dead and dying race, Jesus had come to die for our sins, and after he died, to rise again. The miracle also shows that Jesus has the power to bring *us* back to life.

OBSERVING THE TEXT

3. What do you notice about the *personal* interactions Jesus has in 7:1–17 with both the centurion (albeit from a distance) and the widow whose son has died? How does he relate to grieving and troubled people?

Eases sorrow   Empathetic

4. What concern seems to lie behind the question that John's disciples ask Jesus (7:19)? What should make the answer to that question obvious to Luke's readers, given what we have just seen Jesus accomplish in 7:1–17?

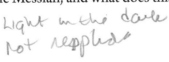
body of faith
more prophede signs

5. How does Jesus talk about John the Baptist in 7:24–28? What is his tone and attitude regarding John? How does he relate John's ministry both to God's promises from the Old Testament and to the coming of the Messiah, and what does this tell us about the role John is playing?

Light in the dark
not reapplied

UNDERSTANDING THE TEXT

6. What does Luke tell us about the character of the centurion? What do the Jews tell Jesus about this man, and what does this reveal about what kind of leader he is (7:1–5)?

Faith

7. What beliefs about Jesus does the centurion reveal through the words
   that he sends to him (7:6–8)? What does he believe that Jesus can
   accomplish? How does Jesus respond—and what does he note about
   the faith of this man?

   All faith. Doesn't need physical

8. What details in Luke's narrative reveal the care that Jesus showed by
   raising the widow's son to life (7:11–14)? What should encourage us
   today about the way that Jesus responds to this widow—as well as to
   the pain of death?

   All temporary

9. What aspect of Jesus's power and purpose does this stunning healing of
   the widow's son serve to highlight (7:15–17)? What kind of authority
   does Jesus demonstrate in this account—and what does it foreshadow
   about what will happen to Jesus himself (and to us)?

   total Authority   Belief in Him

Faith Matters, pg. 313

By the same word that once created the universe out of nothing, and
that now brings sinners from darkness into light, Jesus delivered the
centurion's servant from death. He did this because the centurion
trusted in his power to heal. This serves as an example of a basic
principle for our own salvation: we will not be healed by the worthiness
of our works, but only by the trust of our faith.

10. What doubts seem to be plaguing John the Baptist and causing him
to send messengers to Jesus (7:18–20)? Why might this be? To what
works and signs does Jesus point John's messengers as a confirmation
of his identity and purpose (7:21–23)?

Who truly he is, Works from a distance

11. How does Jesus explain the significance of John's work and ministry to
the crowds who have gathered around him (7:24–30)? What response
should all people of faith have to both the prophetic words of John and
the powerful ministry of Jesus (7:31–35)? Why did many people reject
both John's ministry and the coming of Jesus?

*Start of faith,
No Beginning*

BIBLE CONNECTIONS

12. In 1 Thessalonians 4:16–17, the apostle Paul writes about the glorious
future that awaits followers of Jesus Christ. Read those verses now. How
does Jesus's miracle in Luke 7 of raising the widow's son to life give us
a glimpse, or hint, of what is coming for all who put their faith in him?

13. Read Isaiah 26:19; 29:18; and 35:5–6. What are these verses describing—and what expectations do they create about the salvation that God will bring through his Messiah? What is Jesus saying to John the Baptist by echoing these promises from Isaiah in his answer to him?

THEOLOGY CONNECTIONS

14. Although Jesus heals the centurion's servant, he does not heal *every* sick person in the land of Israel. He also raises the widow's son from the dead, but this does not serve as the young man's final resurrection—he will die again. How do these simple reminders point to the ultimate *purpose* for which Jesus performs his healings and miracles? What is he seeking to teach, through them, about his identity—and about the greater healing that lasts for eternity and comes to those who have faith in him?

15. The Westminster Confession of Faith teaches that, after death, "the souls of the righteous, being then made perfect in holiness, are received into the highest heavens, where they behold the face of God in light and glory, waiting for the full redemption of their bodies" (32.1). How do Jesus's actions in Luke 7:1–17 hint at the "full redemption" of the bodies of all who put their faith in him?

APPLYING THE TEXT

16. What do you learn about Jesus's heart from the healing of the centurion's servant? From the raising of the widow's son? How should the stunning faith of the centurion serve as a model for the way you should trust the power of Jesus's authoritative word to rule over your life and guide you each day?

    all is possible

17. How can Luke's account of how Jesus raised the widow's son inform your perspective on death and your hope in the resurrection? How can this passage serve to encourage you when you are faced with the death of friends or loved ones?

18. What doubts do you still struggle with regarding Jesus's power, identity, or purposes within the world or for your life? What do you do with your doubts—and where do you turn? How can Jesus's answer to John the Baptist's own doubts encourage you to trust him more deeply?

Looking at Jesus, pg. 330
The way to know for sure whether Jesus is the Christ is to go back to his person and work. This is what we should always do when God fails to meet our expectations, when we are overwhelmed by our personal problems and plagued with doubt. We need to go back to Jesus and look again to see who he is and what he does.

PRAYER PROMPT

You have been studying a passage that calls you, as a follower of Jesus, to consider his power, his authority, his compassion, and his true identity: the Christ from God. As you close your study today, thank God for sending his Son—a Savior who is full of compassion and healing—through whom you have the hope of spiritual healing and of resurrection from the dead. Pray that God would enable you to trust in Jesus, even during seasons of doubt, uncertainty, and confusion—and ask him to give you the faith to take him at his word!

LESSON 10

A WOMAN FORGIVEN

Luke 7:36–8:56; 10:38–42

THE BIG PICTURE

For this lesson, you will focus on one passage (Luke 7:36–8:3) while also briefly studying a related passage (Luke 10:38–42). Both of them highlight women who respond to Jesus's grace and mercy with faith, love, and devotion. Luke holds up these beautiful women of faith as examples for all believers who seek to respond to Jesus humbly and worshipfully as well.

Jesus is reclining at dinner at the home of a Pharisee named Simon when something unexpected happens: a woman who is well known around the city (and is probably a prostitute) enters the room, approaches Jesus, pours out a jar of expensive perfume onto his feet, and wipes his feet with her hair while washing them with her tears (7:36–38). The dinner guests are indignant, but Jesus shows them how this woman's response is a picture of right love, devotion, and worship being given to the Christ (7:39–50). He does so by telling a parable about two debtors—one who owes a large sum of money and the other of whom owes a lesser sum. Simon himself has to admit that the one who owes the larger sum will respond with greater love if his debt is forgiven (v. 43). This forgiven woman, who has responded to Jesus's grace with love and worship, leaves the dinner as Jesus commends her faith-filled response (7:50). Luke then adds a brief description of the other women who have followed Jesus, in which he names them and notes their faithful devotion to him (8:1–3).

After this, as chapter 8 goes on, Jesus continues teaching, both explicitly and through parables, as well as reinforcing his teaching with miracles that demonstrate the power and authority he has over creation, the demonic realm, disease, and even death itself (8:4–56).

The second passage that this lesson will cover portrays Mary's and Martha's contrasting responses to Jesus when he visits with them (10:38–42). When Martha grows frustrated with Mary, who is sitting at Jesus's feet in order to learn from him, Jesus gently rebukes her for busily obsessing over cleaning and preparations. Mary, according to Jesus, has chosen the better response to him—not merely busily *serving* him but *sitting* at his feet in admiration, worship, and love.

Read Luke 7:36–8:56 and 10:38–42.

GETTING STARTED

1. What kinds of people do you tend to view as being *beyond* the reach of God's grace and salvation? Why is this the case?

   Sin no more

2. What tends to distract you the most from your relationship with God and your worship of Jesus Christ? How do you find even *good* pursuits and tasks getting in the way of your worship, prayer, and meditation on God?

Great Debt, Great Forgiveness, Great Love, pg. 347

It is the forgiven who make the best lovers. The more people have been forgiven, the more they love, as even Simon had to admit. So what did the woman's passion for Jesus say about her? It proved that the great debt of her sin had been forgiven.

OBSERVING THE TEXT

3. Note the words of rebuke that Jesus speaks in these passages. How does he rebuke Simon—and why? How does he rebuke Martha—and why?

Pay attn   Paul Harvey

4. What prominent roles do women play in both of the passages we are reading and studying for this lesson? Why do you think Luke chooses to feature women so prominently in them? How does the focus on women in these passages bear out Luke's purpose for writing his gospel as well as the emphasis that it contains throughout?

5. In what ways do these passages anticipate the ultimate saving work that Christ will accomplish through his death on the cross? How does the cross validate the words of grace, forgiveness, and mercy that Jesus speaks to sinners?

UNDERSTANDING THE TEXT

6. What do you notice about how Luke introduces the woman who approaches Jesus, as well as about the internal reaction that Simon has to her (7:36–40)? What do these details tell us about the character and condition of this woman?

    Johnson

7. Why is telling a parable an apt and powerful way to rebuke Simon after his response to the woman who has just washed Jesus's feet with perfume and tears (7:41–43)? What point is Jesus making through this parable that he uses to teach Simon?

8. What motivation does Jesus identify behind the woman's passionate and sacrificial act of worship toward him (7:44–47)? What does he promise her about her sins, and what makes this a significant statement about his identity and authority—one that leads to questions from the dinner guests (7:48–50)?

Grace Test, pg. 345

One way to test our grasp of God's grace is to see how we respond to the people we think of as sinners. What we say about them, how we treat them, and what we do (or fail to do) to touch their lives with the love of Jesus Christ indicate our true understanding of God and his grace.

9. Why might Luke have chosen to include the list of women in this passage who accompanied Jesus during his ministry (8:1–3)? What do you notice about the work Jesus has done in their lives and about the way that they support him in his ministry?

10. What might initially tempt us to sympathize with the frustration that Martha shows with Mary (10:38–42)? But what, according to Jesus, is "better" about the choice that Mary has made?

11. What aspects of true faith do we see within these two passages? What are they teaching us about the right way for people to respond to Jesus who have been forgiven and want to follow him passionately?

Sunday Morning christons
true faith

BIBLE CONNECTIONS

12. Read 1 John 1:9, and note God's beautiful promise for those who confess their sin and turn to Jesus in faith. How does Jesus apply the truth of this promise to the woman in Luke 7—and what makes him ultimately able to back up this promise and secure her salvation?

13. In 1 Peter 4:9–10, the apostle Peter tells us to use our gifts—and specifically the gift of hospitality—for the good of others. Read those verses now. While Jesus is not accusing Martha in Luke 10 of sinning in conjunction with her service and hospitality, he is seeking to teach her where her focus should lie while she is serving. What is he helping her to see—and how could this teaching apply to us today?

THEOLOGY CONNECTIONS

14. Sin has corrupted everyone in the world and made us all entirely fallen and utterly in need of God's saving grace. The Westminster Confession of Faith puts it this way: "We are utterly indisposed, disabled, and made opposite to all good, and wholly inclined to all evil" (6.4). Why is it important for us to see our own sin and fallenness as being equal to the sin of the woman in Luke 7? How should understanding our sin and need in this light cause us to be even more stunned and amazed by the forgiveness and grace that Jesus has shown us?

15. The doctrine of justification by faith alone is central to the Reformed tradition—and is absolutely crucial to a right understanding of the gospel of Jesus Christ. How does Jesus's response to the sinful woman in this passage illustrate the truth and the beauty of this doctrine? Consider Philip Ryken's observation that "the woman did not earn forgiveness

by her love. No, the point of the parable and of everything else Jesus said to Simon was that her love was the proof of her prior forgiveness."[1]

APPLYING THE TEXT

16. How can what these passages show you about Jesus's heart serve to encourage your faith and deepen your love for him? How should the loving and gentle care that we see Jesus showing to women in these passages, and the relationships that he has with them, shape the way in which the church values and respects women?

17. Have you been guilty of responding to others the way that Simon the Pharisee responded to the woman in Luke 7:39? How so? How could deepening your understanding of the measureless grace that God has shown *you* shape the way you respond to other sinful people who need his grace?

Prayer while serving

1. Philip Graham Ryken, *Luke*, vol. 1, *Chapters 1–12* (Phillipsburg, NJ: 2009), 349–50.

18. Have you been "distracted with much serving" in your relationship with Jesus (10:40)? How so? While not losing sight of the fact that we are called to obey and serve him, what could you do to slow down and take time to worship, meditate on Jesus's goodness, and sit at his feet as Mary did?

PRAYER PROMPT

As you reflect on the two pictures of worshipful devotion to the gracious Savior that these passages portray, spend some time praying that God would enable you to respond to Jesus as these women did. Ask him for the humility to grasp the depth of the mercy that God has shown you, a sinner, through his Son. Pray for him to give you the focus to sit at Jesus's feet so that you can spend time with him, learn from his Word, and prayerfully consider his goodness and grace.

Choosing the Good Portion, pg. 563

When we make this kind of time for Jesus—quality time to meet him in his Word and through prayer—we are choosing the good portion. Jesus is the perfect antidote for all the unattractive attitudes that poison our service when we turn our attention away from him. His gospel is the cure for our distraction, as we are drawn to the beauty of his grace.

LESSON 11

THE COST OF DISCIPLESHIP

Luke 9:1–62

THE BIG PICTURE

The passage you will study in this lesson is packed with activity and contains a number of events that Luke records from Jesus's public ministry. As he does so, he focuses in particular—as will this lesson—on the way Jesus teaches and prepares his disciples to understand him rightly, follow him obediently, and proclaim him faithfully to the world. Jesus's disciples follow a Messiah who will suffer and die in order to bring salvation to God's people, and they are called to follow him in the path of suffering—the way of the cross. There will be an eternal reward for following Jesus, but this discipleship will involve a cost as well. This passage contains a verse—Luke 9:51—that serves as a pivot point within Luke's gospel and shows Jesus setting his face toward Jerusalem. The Messiah, before receiving eternal glory, must first go to the cross.

The chapter opens with Jesus sending out his disciples to preach and heal, on his behalf, in the villages surrounding Jerusalem—as even Herod seeks to see and hear more about him (9:1–9). After Jesus miraculously feeds a crowd of five thousand people (9:10–17), Peter offers a remarkably clear confession that Jesus is the Christ of God (9:18–20). Jesus then quickly clarifies both the saving *work* of the Christ and the *way* of the cross that his followers must embrace (9:21–27). Jesus will be crucified—and his disciples must prepare to take up their own crosses as they follow him. After Peter, James, and John are shown a vision of Jesus's eternal and ultimate

95

glory on the Mount of Transfiguration (9:28–36), we find that the disciples have still not reached a full faith in and understanding of Jesus. They fail to cast out a demon and then argue about who is the greatest, even as Jesus *again* hints at his coming suffering and death as well as telling them that whoever is not against them is for them (9:37–50). Jesus's eyes then turn toward Jerusalem as he begins preparing for the central aspect of his work on earth: the cross (9:51–56). The passage concludes as Jesus confronts several potential disciples with the great cost of following him—for Jesus's followers as well as himself, the cross will come before the crown (9:57–62).

Read Luke 9:1–62.

GETTING STARTED

1. What are some wrong expectations that you have had in the past regarding following Jesus? What role has your understanding of suffering played in your walk with the Lord and your faith in Jesus Christ?

2. Why does the ability to practice delayed gratification help us in general to succeed in life? How does this concept play in to a right understanding of the gospel and of the path of discipleship that those who want to follow Jesus must take?

Never Look Back, pg. 508

In the same way that Jesus once set his face toward Jerusalem, God is calling us to set our hearts on Jesus and follow him. Look to Jesus, the Scripture says, "who for the joy that was set before him endured the cross, despising the shame, and is seated at the right hand of the throne of God" (Heb. 12:2). Look to Jesus, and never look back.

OBSERVING THE TEXT

3. What consistent themes and ideas do you observe throughout the teaching and instructions that Jesus delivers to his disciples in this passage? How does he allude to his suffering and death—as well as to his ultimate glory and victory?

4. At what points in this passage do Jesus's disciples respond positively and obediently to him? Conversely, what evidence do you find that they have not yet fully grasped what his purpose is—or what their calling is as his disciples?

5. What other responses to Jesus —both positive and negative—do you observe throughout this passage?

UNDERSTANDING THE TEXT

6. What makes it evident that Jesus is entrusting his disciples with significant responsibility and power as he sends them out in 9:1–6? How does he tell them to respond to people who reject them? How would you describe the way that Herod responds to what he hears about Jesus, and what do we learn from his response (9:7–9)?

7. What is so encouraging about Peter's confession of Jesus's identity (9:18–20)? Is it theologically accurate? Why do you think Jesus immediately follows Peter's confession by teaching about his death (9:21–22)? What will Jesus's suffering and death mean for his followers and the path of discipleship that they must walk after him (9:23–27)?

8. How does the transfiguration that Peter, James, and John witness point to Jesus's identity as well as his ultimate glory and victory (9:28–36)? What does it remind us about his suffering as well as his eternal destiny as the Son of God?

9. In the four passages that follow this transfiguration account, what key indications do you see that the disciples have not yet fully grasped the suffering and death that lie ahead for Jesus—or their own call to follow the way of the cross (9:37–50)?

The Gospel of the Crucifixion, pg. 451

Peter's confession of the Christ is the climax (to this point) of Luke's Gospel. Thus it would seem like a moment to celebrate. After months of training, the disciples finally understood who Jesus was. Surely it was time for them to rejoice in Jesus as the Christ, and for Jesus to praise them for their profound understanding of his person. Instead, Jesus immediately began preaching to them the gospel of his crucifixion and resurrection.

10. Many scholars identify Luke 9:51 as a key transitional verse within the gospel of Luke. Why do you think that is? What does it mean that Jesus "set his face" toward Jerusalem? What does this verse remind us regarding Jesus's ultimate purpose on earth as the Messiah?

11. In Luke 9:57–62, we see potential disciples expressing interest in following Jesus. What is similar about the response he gives to each one? What is he teaching them about the cost and requirements that those who truly follow him as his disciples will face?

BIBLE CONNECTIONS

12. Read Philippians 2:1–11. How does Paul describe both the humiliation and the exaltation of Jesus Christ in this passage? In what way does he say that these things should serve as a model for the attitudes and actions adopted by Christ's disciples?

13. Read Acts 5:41, in which Luke records how the apostles respond to being flogged for preaching the gospel of Jesus Christ. What has changed about the apostles' understanding of the purpose of both Christ's suffering and their own, between Luke 9 and Acts 5?

THEOLOGY CONNECTIONS

14. Jesus explicitly says in John's gospel, shortly after miraculously feeding a crowd of five thousand people, that he is the "bread of life" (John 6:35). How does that miracle foreshadow the way Jesus's body will be broken on the cross in order to give life to God's people? How might this help us to understand what we are celebrating, and partaking in, when we take the Lord's Supper?

15. The Westminster Confession of Faith explains that Jesus endured the suffering of the cross willingly: "This office the Lord Jesus did most willingly undertake, which, that he might discharge, he was made under the law, and did perfectly fulfill it; endured most grievous torments immediately in his soul, and most painful sufferings in his body" (8.4). How does this passage that we have been studying affirm his willingness to endure the suffering of the cross for the sake of God's people?

APPLYING THE TEXT

16. What about Jesus's purpose do the disciples fail to see in this passage—
    and how do you see your own mistakes and confusion reflected in some
    of their failures to understand and have faith? What makes it difficult for
    you to embrace suffering, humility, and hardship as you follow Jesus?

17. How does the cross of Jesus Christ free you to suffer gladly for him?
    How can the suffering that he endured in your place provide you with
    the motivation to endure hardship as his disciple?

18. In what sense is your relationship with God and discipleship under
    Jesus *costly* for you? Are there ways in which God might be calling you
    to take up your cross more intentionally, sacrificially, or joyfully for the
    glory of Jesus?

Serious Choices, pg. 464
The tradeoff of discipleship forces us to make some serious choices.
Will we follow Jesus, or go our own way? Will we take up our cross, or
leave it behind? Will we keep our lives for ourselves, or give them away
for Jesus? The decisions we make determine our destiny.

PRAYER PROMPT

At the center of this passage we have studied is the vision of the transfigured and glorified Jesus Christ, which tells us that the Messiah—along with those who repent and put their faith in him—will ultimately be victorious and exalted to all glory and power. The crown is coming—for both Jesus and his people! In the meantime, however, his disciples are called to follow in the way of the cross as they worship a Savior who endured crucifixion in order to secure their salvation. Today, pray that God will help you to be willing to follow Jesus along the path of costly discipleship as you worship him. Ask God to give you humility, as well as a deeper love for his Son, as you devote yourself entirely to his kingdom.

LESSON 12

ON MISSION WITH JESUS

Luke 10:1–24

THE BIG PICTURE

The previous lesson showed us Jesus preparing his disciples, who did not yet understand the Messiah's identity and purpose—and particularly his path of suffering and death. Jesus Christ will be eternally glorified, but he will first set his face toward Jerusalem and the cross; and he invites his disciples to follow him in the way of the cross after they have counted the great cost of discipleship.

Luke 10 begins as Jesus commissions a different group of seventy-two disciples, whom he sends out so they can bear witness to him throughout the towns of Israel and proclaim that, in Christ, the kingdom of God has come near (10:1–12). It seems that this group does *not* include Jesus's twelve disciples but is made up of other men and women who have been following him and who seek to make known the good news of his coming. Jesus instructs them not only to proclaim the good news of the kingdom but also to declare judgment on the towns that reject their message about the Messiah who has come (vv. 10–12). He goes on to speak of the devastating judgment that will come to those who reject him and his message—since they are rejecting not merely a prophet of God, as of old, but God's Son in the flesh (10:13–16).

When the seventy-two followers of Jesus return, they are rejoicing in the authority that his power has given them over demons (10:17–20). Jesus indicates that this authority is indeed a sign of his victory and of Satan's defeat, though he says that the main cause of their rejoicing should be that they have been accepted into God's family through their faith in him. He explains to his disciples the significance of what they have seen—God revealing his Son to the world and many people turning to him in faith (10:21–24). We, ourselves, have been sent out by Jesus on the mission of proclaiming his life-giving gospel to a dying world, as well.

Read Luke 10:1–24.

GETTING STARTED

1. Why are Christians today sometimes tempted to view Jesus's twelve disciples as larger-than-life heroes of the faith? Why is it important for us to remember that they were very human and were sinners saved by grace, just as we are?

2. What makes it tempting for us to embrace the *grace* of Jesus without committing ourselves to the *mission* of Jesus? What challenges arise when we actively seek to make the good news of the gospel known in our social circles, neighborhoods, and families?

Important Instructions, pg. 512

As Jesus sent out these seventy-two evangelists to do gospel work in word and deed, he gave them some very specific instructions. These instructions show the priority of prayer, the presence of danger, the promise of provision, the peace of welcoming the kingdom, and the peril of rejecting it.

OBSERVING THE TEXT

3. What does Jesus's sending of this group of seventy-two indicate about gospel ministry and the proclamation of the kingdom of God? Why is it significant that he commissions a broader group than his twelve disciples?

4. What effects does this group's ministry have? What is immediately encouraging to them as they proclaim the kingdom of God—and how does Jesus respond to their excitement? What does his response reveal about his priorities?

5. How does Jesus teach his disciples throughout this passage about the significance of his *coming* as well as about the importance of his identity and all that it means for God's kingdom on earth?

UNDERSTANDING THE TEXT

6. What priority and purpose does Jesus ascribe to the work and message of the seventy-two in his initial instructions to them (10:1–5)? What are they to leave behind—and what are they to focus on?

7. What different responses does Jesus tell his followers to anticipate from different towns—and what are they to do when they encounter these different responses (10:6–12)? What does this help us to understand about the different types of responses we may get from people when we share the gospel message?

8. Why does Jesus speak such harsh words of judgment against the towns and people of his day who reject him (10:13–16)? What do we learn from these verses about Jesus's close association with his gospel messengers?

9. What makes it evident that Jesus's power is present with the messengers he has sent out (10:17–19)? What does he say should cause them to rejoice even more than they do over their spiritual power and victory (10:20)?

A Sober Warning, pg. 520

This is a sober warning for anyone who hears the good news about Jesus Christ but refuses to receive him as Savior and King. God holds us responsible for whatever we know about Jesus Christ: the greater the opportunity, the greater our responsibility. Whenever the gospel is preached, the kingdom of God is near.

10. What does Jesus teach us in Luke 10:21–22 about his identity, power, and authority? To whom does he say the Father has chosen to reveal his Son? What should this teach us about the right, humble, and faithful way to respond to the gospel?

11. In Luke 10:23–24, what does Jesus tell the disciples about the moment they are experiencing in the history of God's plan for the world? Why is the coming of the Messiah so central to that plan—and why would the prophets and kings from Israel's past have longed to see the day that the disciples are now seeing?

BIBLE CONNECTIONS

12. Skim through Genesis 19, which records the shocking sinfulness of the city of Sodom and the fiery judgment that God sends from heaven against its citizens. What is striking about the mention Jesus makes of Sodom in Luke 10:12? What does this verse teach us about the culpability of those who hear the good news about Jesus Christ and yet reject it?

13. Read Revelation 12:9–11, in which John describes the glorious victory Christ won against Satan when he threw him down from heaven. What reference does Jesus himself make to his powerful triumph over Satan in this passage from Luke (see 10:18)? What makes his words, and John's description of his vision, such good news for the people of God?

THEOLOGY CONNECTIONS

14. In 1973, the Presbyterian Church in America was formed for the purpose of being a denomination that would be "faithful to the Scriptures, true to Reformed doctrine, and obedient to the Great Commission." Many other denominations around the world similarly combine a commitment to biblical doctrine with a passionate devotion to evangelism and mission. How does the passage we are studying today support these commitments?

15. Answer 29 of the Westminster Larger Catechism teaches the following about the eternal judgment of those who reject Christ and his gospel: "The punishments of sin in the world to come, are everlasting separation from the comfortable presence of God, and most grievous torments in soul and body, without intermission, in hell-fire forever." What does Jesus say in this lesson's passage about this final judgment and about who will fall under it? To whom does he say eternal life is made available?

APPLYING THE TEXT

16. What does this passage teach you about the responses that you should anticipate to the gospel of Jesus Christ as you proclaim it to those around you? How should you handle rejection from those who do not want to follow Jesus? Are they rejecting you personally? Why is it important to understand whom you are representing as you share the gospel?

Lunch Room

17. How can this passage give you the energy to undertake Jesus's mission in both your words and your deeds? What from your study of this lesson should motivate you to carry his love and truth to the world around you?

18. Jesus tells the exultant group of seventy-two to rejoice more over their acceptance into God's family than over the victorious deeds they have performed against the demons (10:20). What does this passage tell you about the *joy* that you are meant to feel in the gracious salvation you have received from God through your faith in his Son? What can you do to nurture that joy?

Will You Share the Message? pg. 521
There is something desperately urgent for everyone to do. People are dying and going to heaven or hell every day. What will you do with the message you have received from the King? How will you labor to share it with others?

PRAYER PROMPT

Although Jesus's commissioning of the seventy-two took place two thousand years ago, he issues his followers today the same call to mission. We are invited by our gracious Savior to believe in him as the Son of God and to proclaim the gospel of his kingdom to the world around us. Today, pray for the courage and faithfulness to bear witness to your Savior in both your words and your deeds. Ask him for understanding and patience as you proceed with the recognition that the gospel message will be accepted by some but rejected by others. Finally, pray that your joy in your gracious Savior will continue to deepen—your Savior who invites you, when you have faith in him, into the family of God for all eternity.

LESSON 13

THE GOOD SAMARITAN

Luke 10:25–37

THE BIG PICTURE

The passage we will study for this final lesson from the first half of Luke
is one of the most well-known parables from Jesus to be found throughout
all the Gospels: the parable of the good Samaritan. Many of the central
themes and emphases of Luke's gospel meet within this parable. It shows
Jesus emphasizing sacrificial, cross-shaped love and service. It portrays
Luke's focus on the outsider—in this case a Samaritan (someone hated by
the Jewish people) who serves as the model of a Christlike love for one's
neighbor. In it we read of the compassion and mercy of this Samaritan man
and as a result are shown the heart of Jesus, whose own compassion and
mercy for weak and wounded sinners is fully revealed at the cross. In an
ironic twist, the true example of God-honoring neighborly love and mercy
has been provided by the most unlikely person!

Jesus tells this parable after being approached by a Jewish lawyer, who
asks him what he must do to inherit eternal life (10:25). When Jesus asks
him what the core of God's law is, the lawyer responds well by summa-
rizing God's law as being the call to love both God and one's neighbor
(10:26–28). But the lawyer's follow-up question—"Who is my neighbor?"
(10:29)—leads Jesus to tell this world-famous parable. In it, a man on the
road to Jericho is robbed and badly beaten and then left to die by the road
(10:30). A Jewish priest and a Levite both pass by the man without helping him in any way (10:31–32). But a Samaritan—a man from a people

group who are generally hated by the Jews—stops to assist the beaten man (10:33–35). He binds his wounds, takes him to an inn, and pays for his care and protection. Jesus invites the young lawyer to identify the Samaritan as being the true merciful neighbor in this parable; he then calls him to act in the same way (10:36–37).

Read Luke 10:25–37.

GETTING STARTED

1. Which people in your life are you able to love and serve most easily and readily? Why is that? Which people—or which *kinds* of people—do you find most difficult to love and serve? Why?

   *ONES WHO RTN FEELINGS / FEELS GOOD Appro
   DIFFICULT AGRESSIVE, CONFRONTATIONAL
   Challenge   Leader*

2. What internal justification have you come up with for certain behaviors that you later came to recognize as being sinful, selfish, or unwise? Why are our hearts particularly adept at justifying our own behaviors and failures while often harshly judging the behaviors and failures of others?

   VIEW OUR EFFORTS OK

Loving Grace for Lawbreakers, pg. 549

The story of the good Samaritan is a law parable, therefore, that shows us how much we need the love God has for us in the gospel. The good news of the gospel is that through the death and resurrection of Jesus Christ, God has loving grace for law-breaking sinners who are not good neighbors. As we read about the good Samaritan, we cannot help but be reminded of the saving work of Jesus Christ, who always practiced what he preached.

OBSERVING THE TEXT

3. What does Luke tell us about the lawyer who approaches Jesus—and
   what questions are you left with, about him, as he is introduced? What
   does he show us that the man understands correctly about God . . . and
   that he does not yet understand?

   IN HIS OWN

4. What is significant about the characters that Jesus includes in the parable that he tells? How do their actions demonstrate what their hearts
   are like—both toward God and toward others?

5. How does Jesus conclude his interaction with the lawyer? What questions might the lawyer have been left with after this interaction with
   him—and what might he have been challenged to change regarding
   his approach to God and to others?

   PARABLE   MORE   INCLUS.

UNDERSTANDING THE TEXT

6. Why does the lawyer's question seem to be good and valid—at least
   on the surface (10:25)? How does Luke imply that his motivation for
   asking this question is not pure—that the question is not fully sincere?

7. How does the lawyer summarize the law in 10:27? Is his summary accurate? What is Jesus's response to what he says (10:28)?

Who is my Neighbor

8. Why did the lawyer ask Jesus the question that we see him asking next (10:29)? In what way—and why—might he have been seeking to "justify" himself before Jesus? What behaviors and failures on his part might he have been trying to excuse?

Holier than thou
Not a Prophet

9. How might the priest and the Levite in Jesus's parable have rationalized their failure to stop and help the beaten and bruised man on the side of the road (10:30–32)? What is significant about the fact that Jesus chose *those* as the specific occupations of the men who failed to act in love and mercy?

Stations of life and faith

Foolish Motives, pg. 537

As important as this question is, there were some problems with the way the lawyer asked it. One was his motivation. Luke tells us that he was putting Jesus to the test. How foolish it is to test God on his theology, and yet people do the same thing today. Rather than accepting Jesus on his own terms, believing that he is the Son of God and Savior of sinners, they evaluate him according to the principles of their own theology.

10. What might have surprised Jesus's audience about the fact that he selected a Samaritan man to be the hero of this story (10:33–35)? How do we see the good Samaritan demonstrating remarkably costly love, compassion, and mercy to the man in need? In what ways do his actions serve as a picture of Jesus's costly love and care for sinners?

11. By verse 36, how has Jesus subtly changed the question that the lawyer asked him? What makes Jesus's final conclusion so clear, profound, and powerful (10:37)?

BIBLE CONNECTIONS

12. Read Leviticus 21:1–3—an Old Testament passage that the Levite in this parable might have had in his mind when he passed by the man who appeared to be dead . . . or at least nearly dead! What should have made his love of God and of his neighbor transcend the ceremonial law in this case? What other passages in the Gospels could be seen as teaching God's people to adopt a similar priority (see Matthew 23:23–24, for example)?

13. In Matthew 5:46–48, Jesus describes the ease with which we love those who love us and issues the radical gospel call for us to love our enemies. Read those verses and then explain how the Samaritan in Jesus's parable beautifully exemplifies the call that they contain. What about the relationship between Jews and Samaritans makes this surprising?

THEOLOGY CONNECTIONS

14. Luke tells us that the lawyer desires to "justify himself" through his response to Jesus after Jesus affirms his summary of the law (10:29). Most likely he is seeking to excuse his failure to love *everyone* as his neighbor, in order to preserve his self-image of being right and good in the eyes of God. Why is any attempt to justify ourselves before God by our works a hopeless one? How does Jesus's parable point to God's compassion and mercy for sinners? Why must the service we perform for God and others always begin with our repenting and trusting in Jesus's grace?

15. The Westminster Shorter Catechism explains in answer 68 that the sixth commandment "requires all lawful endeavors to preserve our own life, and the life of others." Following their typical pattern, the Westminster divines interpret each of the Ten Commandments as teaching both prohibitions and positive commands. How does the Samaritan clearly and beautifully fulfill the positive demand of God's law not to commit murder but instead to protect life?

APPLYING THE TEXT

16. What aspects of the lawyer's questioning of—and attitude toward—Jesus do you see in your own heart? In what sense are you guilty of seeking to excuse yourself from loving certain kinds of people? In what ways do you seek to justify your own behavior in order to preserve *your* self-image of being a "good" person who can earn God's favor?

17. How should this parable that Jesus tells drive you to the hope of the gospel? In what ways could you interpret this parable as being a metaphor of your own salvation?

18. Jesus follows his parable with a simple command that he gives to the lawyer: "You go, and do likewise" (10:37). How is this parable challenging you, personally, to love your own neighbors? In what ways do you need to strengthen your costly compassion for, mercy toward, and generosity to others?

Showing Mercy, pg. 551
Do not cross over to the other side, but take the time to stop and help. Do not quit before the job is done, but by the grace of God, carry things all the way through. Do not do these things to gain eternal life, but because when you were beaten, bloodied, and left for dead, Jesus came and showed mercy to you.

PRAYER PROMPT

As you reflect on this beautiful and convicting parable that Jesus has told, respond to it first by remembering the merciful and compassionate work that Jesus Christ has done on your behalf. Thank him that *he* is the ultimate good Samaritan—the one who cares for you eternally through his saving work on the cross, where he was bloodied and beaten in your place. Then pray for God to give you a heart like Jesus's, as you seek to love your neighbors—all of them—mercifully, compassionately, and sacrificially.

Jon Nielson is senior pastor of Spring Valley Presbyterian Church in Roselle, Illinois, and the author of *Bible Study: A Student's Guide*, among other books. He has served in pastoral positions at Holy Trinity Church, Chicago, and College Church, Wheaton, Illinois, and as director of training for the Charles Simeon Trust.

Philip Graham Ryken (DPhil, University of Oxford) is president of Wheaton College. He teaches the Bible for the Alliance of Confessing Evangelicals, speaking nationally on the radio program *Every Last Word*, and is the author of a number of books and commentaries.

P&R PUBLISHING'S COMPANION COMMENTARY

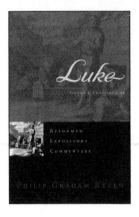 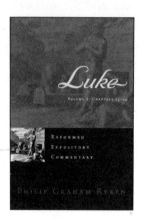

In this commentary, Philip Graham Ryken makes Luke's message clear for a contemporary audience by explaining, illustrating, and applying its truth to everyday life, with the hope that readers will understand the gospel and come to full assurance of salvation, as Luke intended. If an account of Jesus's life was needed in Luke's time, how much more acutely is it needed in ours—and Luke's gospel stands as ready as ever to fill this need.

The Reformed Expository Commentary (REC) series is accessible to both pastors and lay readers. Each volume in the series provides exposition that gives careful attention to the biblical text, is doctrinally Reformed, focuses on Christ through the lens of redemptive history, and applies the Bible to our contemporary setting.

Praise for the Reformed Expository Commentary Series

"Well-researched and well-reasoned, practical and pastoral, shrewd, solid, and searching." —**J. I. Packer**

"A rare combination of biblical insight, theological substance, and pastoral application." —**Al Mohler**

"Here, rigorous expository methodology, nuanced biblical theology, and pastoral passion combine." —**R. Kent Hughes**